BACK IN THE
GAME

BACK IN THE
GAME

One Gunman, Countless Heroes, and the Fight for My Life

Steve Scalise
with Jeffrey E. Stern

CENTER
STREET®

New York   Nashville

Center Street
Hachette Book Group
1290 Avenue of the Americas, New York, NY 10104
centerstreet.com
twitter.com/centerstreet

First Edition: November 2018

Center Street is a division of Hachette Book Group, Inc. The Center Street name and logo are trademarks of Hachette Book Group, Inc.

The publisher is not responsible for websites (or their content) that are not owned by the publisher.

The Hachette Speakers Bureau provides a wide range of authors for speaking events. To find out more, go to www.HachetteSpeakersBureau.com or call (866) 376-6591.

Library of Congress Cataloging-in-Publication Data has been applied for.

ISBNs: 978-1-5460-7613-1 (hardcover), 978-1-5460-7637-7 (signed edition), 978-1-5460-7636-0 (B&N signed edition), 978-1-5460-7611-7 (ebook)

Printed in the United States of America

LSC-C

10 9 8 7 6 5 4 3 2 1

This book is dedicated to God, for Your guiding force, and for all of the little miracles You performed along the way to give me a second chance at life; to Jennifer, for being our family's rock, and for your strength and love throughout; and to Madison and Harrison, so you can one day know of all the heroes who saved your dad's life.

PROLOGUE

The Whipper-In

At right around 7:00 AM, when the gunman walked up to the baseball practice, I was at second base.

Officer Kevin Jobe of the Alexandria Police Department had just started his patrol; firefighter and paramedic Richard Krimmer was sitting at a kitchen table in Station 207, listening to his battalion chiefs on a conference call.

Special Agents Crystal Griner and David Bailey were in the Suburban parked just off the baseball field, with the windows down and the radio low.

A few miles away, my good friend Cedric Richmond, Democratic Congressman and Chairman of the Congressional Black Caucus, was at the Democrats' practice.

Dr. Jack Sava and Susan Kennedy, of the trauma department at the MedStar Washington Hospital Center, were just about to come on shift.

These people, and many others, would come together over the next few seconds, the next days and months, to bring me back from the brink of death. In that way, the gunshot that marked the start of that attack was actually a starting gun of sorts, for all kinds of different people racing to my side, coming together for the purpose of saving this one grateful man. To make me feel like it wasn't just me but the whole country that had been shot at. I would get to see a nation unified, to see different people from all different backgrounds rooting and praying and working for me to survive.

✛ ✛ ✛

At first, from where I stand, I don't think we're under attack.

After the *bang*, the first thing I see is a tractor, so the first thing I think is *tractor*.

If I register anything it's *Oh, a backfire.*

The notion that we're being attacked—that I am under attack—doesn't fit. It doesn't work; it's dissonant, a glitch, I'm watching a movie with the wrong sound, a horror flick with a laugh track, a comedy with panicky strings. It's a warm and gorgeous day, the grass fresh cut and loamy. I feel the sunbaked vinyl numbers on my jersey, warming my back. I'm flooded by all the sensations you experience when you're smiling and joking with your friends and outside playing a kid's game, and these things don't make sense with gunfire attached to them. It takes me too long, and I'm just standing there, because the notion is too confusing.

Although when I think about it now, this strange melding of opposite things, I realize it's what that whole day, and everything that came after it, was about. It's fitting, really. In the most literal sense, bringing different ideas together is actually my job. I'm the House majority whip, after all, the "whipper-in," a term taken from the old fox chases, where someone had to go after the stray hounds to crack whips and fire rat-shot over their heads to scare them back into the pack. The whipper-in brings together creatures that sometimes stray very far apart. My job is to bring people together to pass bills, to build coalitions, but I've never in my life brought people together as effectively as I did when I was on the brink of death.

That day began a convergence of people from all walks of life, people of very different personal backgrounds and different political inclinations, people who otherwise have had, if we're being honest, very little common cause in recent years. So whether you personally share the same conservative principles I have or subscribe to a much different political philosophy, I hope even the most cynical among you will acknowledge, if only silently and to yourselves, that what this story suggests most of all is that there's something very unique and very powerful about you, about all of us.

You may have heard the story of this baseball shooting and moved on, never having known how seriously some of us were hurt, how close to death we were.

You may not have known how long the road to recovery has been and how much of it still lies ahead. Certainly, there have been many, much bigger tragedies, affecting many more people, since that day.

Still, I—one man struggling to survive—received so much support, and so many prayers, and so many gestures from so many far-flung places, I felt like I was being lifted up by the entire nation. In all the kindness and humor and gifts and prayers pouring into my one little hospital room; in all the talent that was brought to bear for my benefit, I was made to feel that an attack on me was an attack on us all. And I was provided a reminder that this nation is special *because* of how many different kinds of people share it, not in spite of that. It's the reason I'm alive. So I've endeavored to make this a book that can welcome anybody, and perhaps challenge everybody.

On the day I was shot, hundreds of pieces of bullet and bone split apart inside me and took me right up to the brink of death, but it was also a day hundreds of things came together so I could survive. As I've looked back on the past year, I've learned new and interesting and inspiring things about many of these people who saved me. I've learned their many different stories. I've tried to learn who they are, these people who played parts, some small, some almost cinematically large, in saving my life.

And I've decided to try and tell the story through them.

This is not just a story about the hundreds of pieces of metal and bone that almost killed me. It's about the hundreds of new pieces of my life. The new *people* in my life.

And I figure, how better to tell this story? How better to tell the story of all the things that had to go right, the hundreds of little miracles and acts of heroism that had to happen for me to be here telling this story, than through those very special people—the heroes God put in place to make those miracles possible?

The way I see it, it's a very small step toward returning the favor.

But right now, small steps are nothing to scoff at.

BACK IN THE
GAME

5:45 PM, Tuesday, June 13th

THE PARKS DEPARTMENT

On the evening of Tuesday, June 13th, a man wandered onto a baseball field in Alexandria, looking around.

It's a well-kept facility with a slight crown, a gentle rounding toward the middle that helps rainwater drain off the sides. It has the effect of making you feel, when you're standing right next to it, like it rises above you. It makes you feel small.

The air was cooling off, the heat of an early summer day easing away. A late afternoon fog was beginning to lift, moving north toward the Capitol, as parks department staff finished their work. They dragged the field to smooth out the bumps; they laid down fresh chalk on the baselines.

As the man surveyed the field, something caught his eye.

A gate, on the third base side.

It seemed, from where he stood, to be open.

That was asking for trouble. An off-leash dog trotting in to dig up a divot; kids leaving behind a few longneck mementos of their summer vacation.

The man walked over to third base, closed the gate, and locked it.

Then he left for the night.

5:00 AM, Wednesday, June 14th

Wednesday was going to be a good day.

I'm always a little giddy as we get closer to a baseball game, and going into the last day of practice, I was as excited as ever. I feel almost foolishly lucky that I get to play a child's game, to go outside and smell the grass and feel the sun and throw a ball around like a kid.

I get to wear a real baseball uniform. Putting on that uniform is as exciting now as it was back in Little League. Back then it was exciting because when I put on a baseball uniform I felt like a grownup. Now it's exciting because when I put on a uniform it makes me feel like a kid. I would lay that uniform on the bed every night before practice. This time, I'd laid out two uniforms, actually—one for that day, my last day of practice, a University of Louisiana-Lafayette uniform, with the fleur-de-lis and "RAGIN' CAJUNS" across the top.

And one for the big game the next day. I couldn't help it.

Next to those two uniforms, I'd laid out my suit for the day. Not as exciting, but even after practice ended, it was going to be a good day at work, because of a deceptively thorny, politically controversial issue we'd finally solved: red snapper.

I know, it sounds trivial, but fishing is a huge part of the culture down in the Gulf, where I'm from—like baseball, a thing fathers do to bond with their children. For years, a disagreement about overfishing persisted between the Department of Commerce, the state governments, and members of Congress, and with no one agreeing on a solution, eventually

2

the Department of Commerce swooped in and cut the fishing season down to just three days.

For years, congressional leaders from the affected states couldn't agree on a response, so when I decided to take it on, it was against the better judgment of just about everyone whose advice I value. Even the speaker of the House, Paul Ryan, gave me that look when I said I was going for red snapper. That roll of the eyes that says, *Your funeral.*

And yet, over the past few weeks, all the representatives from all the districts affected had gathered in my conference room on the third floor of the Capitol, often after dinner, often staying late into the evening, talking through every single viewpoint, every possible solution, all its merits and unintended consequences. And though it sounds exhausting, really, it's why I love my job: because in Congress, issues like this abound, issues that seem hyper-specific, even silly, but that impact spending bills, land management bills—all kinds of broader, more obviously far-reaching legislation. And of course, there's no such thing as a silly or trivial law to those directly affected by one. But when you put members of Congress in the same room together, feed them, and listen to them, often you can actually forge solutions between people who never thought they could agree on anything.

So, after a lot of late nights debating the finer points of red snapper fishing, we finally landed on an idea everyone could agree on, and forwarded our proposal on to the Commerce Department. The evening before that last practice, Commerce called—we'd convinced them.

I just about hollered. We'd solved red snapper! I felt like

we'd figured out cold fusion. Commerce was set to announce the new policy, so Chris Bond and Lauren Fine, my communications staff, put together a series of press calls for after practice. I was excited. I was proud.

We would announce the breakthrough after practice.

✛ ✛ ✛

That morning, as I rode out from D.C. to the small Virginia ballpark where the team practiced, I had some time to reflect on what—at the time—felt like some of the most important things in life.

I thought about my teammate, Kevin Brady, whose committee was drafting the largest tax reform package since 1986 and who was relying on me to help get the votes to pass it.

I thought about the final details for another meeting I had after practice, about reforming the National Flood Insurance Program.

I daydreamed about the next day, walking into Nationals Park, taking my position as starting second baseman, with my wife, Jennifer, and kids in the stands to cheer me on.

I'd always relished these morning rides to the ballpark, because they were probably the only part of the day I had to myself. That early in the morning, even Horton leaves me alone. Brett Horton, the chief of staff for my whip office, who oversees much of my day-to-day activities and tries to squeeze as much as he can out of every hour. If a meeting is cancelled, it's not a sudden windfall of leisure time to sit in my office and look down the National Mall, pondering its history and all the people who took in the same view, from the same office, before me.

Brett finds a call to fit in or assembles an impromptu meeting in no time flat.

He denies me a few minutes for lunch if I don't mount a convincing argument.

But even Brett, the hyperactive Tetris master of the Outlook calendar, has to leave the 5:00 and 6:00 AM hours alone. No one, in any time zone, wants a meeting or a call at that hour.

So as I rode out to northern Virginia for baseball practice, U2 on the radio, and no calls to make, in my mind, I was back in the 80s, a high schooler driving out to the sandlot for a pickup game with the neighborhood kids.

That drive was just about as peaceful as life got.

✦ ✦ ✦

Players started arriving at around 5:30 AM. It was shaping up to be one of those warm, breezy days that bring a smile to your face and seem to carry your cares up into the clouds. Everything was good. Work was good. Life was good. I felt great. Stepping out onto the field, I was excited about practice, and even more excited about the fact that I would get to see my kids the next day. And after the game, my son Harrison would stay in D.C. for a week. The past couple of years my daughter Madison, who is two years older than my son, had spent a week in the summer with me in Washington, tagging along to meetings, always by my side. Those were incredibly special times for me to bond with my daughter and for her to see what Daddy does whenever he gets on a plane to leave for a few days at a time. This year, Harrison was finally old enough to join me, and I had two tickets to a U2 concert. So out on the field, I was thinking, *What could be better?* I had a few legislative wins behind me, a summer of baseball, father–son bonding, and a raucous concert all lay in front of me.

By 6:00 AM, practice was under way.

By 6:30 AM, we were trash talking, whooping, and zinging the ball around the diamond. Around us, the neighborhood was coming to life. People were jogging, walking their dogs, looking through the chain links to watch us practice.

Soon, more than 30 people were either playing or hanging around the park. The normal weekday throng lined up for their morning fix at Swing's Coffee, across the street.

People were beginning to arrive at the YMCA, next to the field, for morning exercise classes.

The area was getting crowded.

By 7:00 AM, most of us had been at it for an hour. Some of the players started to leave. I knew I probably should too, but I wanted to stay just a little longer. Just field a few more grounders, make a few more throws, before leaving the field, heading home to shower, and to get ready for the day.

5:30 AM

THE GUNMAN

At around the time our team began showing up at the field, an out-of-work home inspector was visiting a storage unit just outside of the city.

He'd been living out of a van in a quiet neighborhood, frequenting a YMCA to use the showers and Wi-Fi.

There, he met the city's former mayor, who took an interest in helping him, and gave him job recommendations and bar recommendations. On the mayor's advice, he started frequenting a barbecue joint down the street, putting on his best khakis and polo shirts and going down to nurse Budweiser and Pabst while the other patrons sipped craft brews.

He watched golf on the bar's TVs. He avoided eye contact. He bothered no one, not deliberately at least, but people noticed him. Bartenders felt a vague sense of unease. He seemed like a strange but probably harmless pensioner, content to quietly while away his afternoons tending to a beer belly and watching golf. He did not talk politics.

At night, alone behind the glow of a laptop screen, he raged. He was roiled by social media, he battled on it, his posts dripping with scorn and hatred toward the Republican Party and President Trump, and the responses to his posts fueled him even more. He was living a kind of double existence. While quiet and unassuming in person, he was angry and confrontational online, a digital flamethrower, a combatant when provided the anonymity of an online avatar.

7

But by June 14th, something had boiled over in him. His hatred spilled from words into action.

He returned 30 minutes after going to the storage shed. He sat in his van with a clear view of the field, watching as I practiced with all my teammates. He could see us clearly. We could not see him.

There, in his van, with the sound of baseballs pinging off aluminum bats in the distance, he could load his weapons without anyone noticing.

It hadn't occurred to any of us that we made an ideal target: A bunch of congressmen gathered in one place, with no cover, and hardly any protection. When members of Congress are away from the Capitol, only the leadership get any kind of security detail—a grand total of 9 people out of 535.

Very few members of leadership have ever gone to the baseball practices.

✤ ✤ ✤

Just after 7:00 AM, Jeff Duncan, a congressman from South Carolina, said he had to leave practice and get to work. He gave me a fist bump and hustled off the field, but before he got to his car, he was stopped by a short, chubby man.

"Excuse me, sir," the man said. "Who's practicing today? Democrats or Republicans?"

"This is a Republican team," Duncan said.

"Okay, thanks."

Then the man turned around and simply walked away, back across the parking lot to his van.

Duncan got in his car and drove away. He thought to himself, *That was odd.*

✢ ✢ ✢

Four minutes later, the man emerged from his van carrying an SKS style semi-automatic rifle with a 40-round banana clip, a fully loaded nine-millimeter Smith & Wesson pistol in a hip holster attached to his waistband, an extra fully loaded 40-round clip for the rifle, and an extra loaded magazine for the pistol—enough ammunition to kill all of us several times over.

He brought his arsenal across the parking lot and toward the baseball field—a big space where a few dozen unsuspecting senators and congressman were fenced in, with virtually no cover. He came toward us, carrying his weapons to the entrance, about to step onto the field and begin his assault—but he couldn't push the gate open.

The gate on the third base side wouldn't budge.

It had been padlocked the night before.

The gunman couldn't get to us. He couldn't get onto the field. For the moment, his plan to walk up to us and begin an all-out assault was stymied.

Then he saw Congressman Trent Kelly from Mississippi on the other side of the fence but just a few feet away, playing third base.

The gunman raised his rifle and aimed right at Trent's head.

✢ ✢ ✢

Trent noticed movement out of the corner of his eye.

He turned just in time to see a rifle barrel pointed directly at him.

Then the man pulled the trigger.

Summer, 2014

THE PEOPLE OF VIRGINIA'S 7TH

The bombshell went off when I was on the way to dinner. It was three years before that fateful baseball practice, almost to the day, and for me it started, as most major moments seem to these days, with a text message.

I was hosting a small dinner with some colleagues at Acadiana, my favorite Cajun restaurant in Washington. It's something I did as a way to unwind, catch up, and learn what other members had on their minds.

On that day, I'd forgotten, or perhaps didn't even know, that some members had primaries.

I didn't even know that Scott Rigell—who was sitting right next to me riding to dinner—had one, until he started checking in by text message with his campaign team.

"You're doing fine," his manager texted him back. "But Eric's in trouble."

Scott glanced over at me. He looked like he'd seen a ghost. "They're saying Eric's in trouble."

Eric who?

Scott's from Virginia. The only "Eric" I could think of from Virginia was Eric Cantor, but it couldn't be Eric Cantor. Eric Cantor was majority leader. He was one of the most powerful politicians in the country and had a nearly unrivaled campaign war chest. There was no way he'd be having any trouble in a *primary*.

I texted Lynnel Ruckert, then my chief of staff. "There's nothing going on in Eric Cantor's primary, is there?"

Her response came quickly. "Actually yeah. Returns are coming in. Something's wrong."

✤ ✤ ✤

Here it's important to point out that even if I'd known that Eric Cantor had an election that day, I still wouldn't have found it worth paying attention to. The latest polling had him winning by 30 points. His opponent had only two paid staffers, raised less than $200,000, didn't even spend all of that, and was running his campaign with a flip-phone. Eric outspent him 40 to 1. Eric was so far ahead he traveled all over the country raising money for *other* members of the party.

Perhaps most important, no majority leader had ever lost a primary. Literally, it had never happened.

At Acadiana, as we sat down to dinner, people were starting to buzz.

Did you hear what's going on in Virginia?

Unbelievable, right?

No way. It can't be.

We were all glued to our phones. With 40% of precincts reporting, Eric was actually losing.

With 50% reporting, the margin widened.

Sixty percent, and the gap was too big to make up.

Just after 8:20 PM, the Associated Press called it: Eric had somehow just become the first majority leader ever to lose a primary.

I was stunned. We all were. Eric is a friend of mine, and a mentor. As we were trying to process those emotions, though, we also all realized, at about the same time, that the party would soon have some big decisions to make. Eric was the House majority leader, and now we knew he'd no longer be in leadership after November. Which meant the party would need a new leader. November wasn't even five months away. The jockeying for position was sure to start soon, maybe even within the next few days.

Tim Griffin, then a congressman from southern Arkansas (now the state's lieutenant governor), was at the dinner, and he turned to me and said, "If Cantor's out, and there's an opening at majority leader, that means there's gonna be an opening at whip."

It was only minutes since polls had closed in Virginia's 7th; that's how fast things were happening.

"Steve," he said, "you should run."

I could hardly wrap my mind around it. I was still addled. I was still shocked. All I could think was, *I need to talk to Jennifer.*

Griffin got more adamant. "Steve, you gotta do it."

I asked the waiter if we could speed up the dinner. More calls were coming in. More people were asking what I was thinking. I needed to call my wife. I needed to confer with my staff. If I was going to even consider trying to make a run, I had no time to waste. Because if I did run, I was going to be running an underdog campaign, compressed into the impossibly short time period of five months.

✛ ✛ ✛

Then five months became eight days.

With the news full of breathless headlines—"ERIC CANTOR AND THE BIGGEST UPSET IN POLITICAL HISTORY," read one *Washington Post* headline; "THE SEISMIC POLITI-CAL CONSEQUENCES OF ERIC CANTOR'S STUNNING LOSS" screamed another—Eric decided not to serve out his term. He'd leave early; he'd resign his position. We weren't losing him in November; we were losing him *immediately*.

And the speaker of the House, John Boehner, didn't want the future of the party's leadership up in the air, not even for five months.

At some point that day, Lynnel called me. "Boss, I'm hear-ing Boehner's calling a snap election."

"Ok. When's it gonna be?"

"It's in eight days."

"It's in *what?!*"

"You gotta make a decision *now*."

I called Jennifer again, and we had a conversation that deserved to span at least a weekend in a few minutes, but Jen's attitude has always been that any sacrifice for the country is one worth making. "Steve, our country needs you more than we do right now. You have to do it. We'll figure it out."

✣ ✣ ✣

I had run one successful internal campaign, to become a cau-cus chairman, but of course I wasn't in leadership, and never had been.

My opponent, Peter Roskam, was the chief deputy whip, next in line to move up to whip. I was going up against an opponent who was not only well liked and a good fundraiser, but also the sitting whip's hand-picked successor (Kevin McCarthy was trying to move up and take over for Eric Cantor).

I was essentially going against the shoe-in.

If I was going to even have a chance, I knew I had to make my case to every single Republican in the House.

I had to talk to 232 people.

In eight days.

Lynnel turned our office into a war room. Brett Horton, who was my policy director at the time, set up shop at the conference table in my office, and together we began mapping out calls. We talked through which issues mattered most to all my colleagues, tried to get them on the phone, then tracked the results of each conversation. Members willing to make calls for me—to join my "whip team"—were really the only supporters I could completely count on, because they were going public with their support.

I worked the phones that first night until well after midnight, until my calls went unanswered, and then went home for a just few hours of sleep so I could get up and be back at it first thing the next day.

Then a complication arose: a spoiler candidate jumped in the race. Marlin Stutzman from Indiana announced he was running.

Now I had two opponents to contend with. A three-way race meant it wasn't likely any one of us could pull more than 50% of the votes, not in just one ballot. Instead, what was likely to happen was that one of us would be eliminated in the first ballot, and the other two would go head-to-head in a runoff.

The plot thickened.

✛ ✛ ✛

I'd never had to be so focused on time management in my life. My staff got it down to a science. Everyone had a role, and under pressure, they were all at peak performance, setting up calls, prepping me on the issues, tracking the results of the calls to try and gauge how much support I actually had.

When my colleagues headed home for Father's Day weekend, I stayed behind. Every single minute I was on the phone with a colleague or waiting to be connected, or, sometimes, both.

When my colleagues returned to D.C. after the weekend, a new opportunity arose: each vote series gave me a captive audience. Each time a vote was called, all the members had to go to the House Chamber, so I'd grab a list of calls I hadn't made yet and head to the floor to track people down.

Meanwhile, the press saw the compressed leadership race as high drama. The normally empty press gallery, a balcony behind the speaker's rostrum where reporters can—but seldom do—watch members of Congress slowly turn the grindstone of democracy, was full to the brim.

My hometown publications were out in force; the state hadn't had anyone in leadership since Hale Boggs was majority leader back in 1971.

This was high pressure.

The lights were on.

This was the Super Bowl. Reporters who'd always ignored me started stalking my moves, yelling out questions as I passed about whether I had the votes.

I didn't.

Sometimes when I approached members on the floor, they'd try to avoid me, turning away like I was an incoming process server, waving a lawsuit. That would get my mind reeling. *I know he saw me. Is he avoiding me because he's already committed to Peter? Does he just think I have no chance? Does he not want to waste his vote on me and just doesn't want to tell me?*

Sometimes I'd see someone on my list across the floor, start moving toward him, and then I'd notice one of my opponents angling in the same direction.

The two of us would pick up the pace, both trying to get there first.

Soon we'd both be powerwalking awkwardly across the floor, two middle-aged men in suits racing across the House Chamber, toward one of the few remaining undecided members. Then, back in my office, we'd read press reports after each vote series about whose hand I'd shaken, who turned away when I approached, and what it meant. It was like reading in-depth analysis in which pundits dissected the political intrigue of a high school dance.

Then I got a boost: the Pennsylvania delegation, which had sworn to vote as a bloc, split. Some of my colleagues from the Keystone State committed to me. I was picking up some momentum. Rumors swirled that Marlin was looking to cut a deal and release his votes. Walking back to my office from a vote series, a reporter hollered at me, "Are you negotiating with your opponents?"

"No deals!" I yelled back as the door shut behind me. I was confident—in retrospect, maybe too confident.

But I couldn't help it. At the moment, I was flying high. The numbers looked good. I felt momentum, and everything was going my way.

Then a setback: Roskam's camp started saying he had all the votes he needed already locked up. If he really did, that meant I didn't. And by then, the vote was only a day away. If Roskam had the votes to win in just one round, it was too late for me to do anything about it.

✛ ✛ ✛

Before the New Orleans Saints played their very first play-off game in the Superdome during the magical 2009–2010 season, head coach Sean Payton gave a pep talk in the locker room. During his speech, he surprised the players with custom-made baseball bats, inscribed with the words:

SAINTS vs CARDINALS.

BRING THE WOOD

JANUARY 16TH 2010

Running back Reggie Bush was so pumped up he ran onto the field holding that bat, and the Saints went on to win the game, then the NFC Championship, then the Super Bowl.

In the closing days of the compressed leadership race in 2014, a friend from back home, Rick Legendre, reminded me of that moment and gave me what I thought was a great idea.

The night before the vote, I gathered everyone on my whip

team for a dinner, back where it all started, at Acadiana. I did it as a kind of rally before the vote and had Roger Williams, a congressman from Texas (but more important, the coach of the congressional baseball team), give a pep talk.

The event was mostly for fun, but there was a little strategy to it as well. Since the next day's vote was a secret ballot, I wanted to bring everyone together, all in one place, so they could see each other, hear each other, feel how big the group really was. It was proof that it wasn't just bluster, that we really had a chance.

As the dinner was wrapping up, before everyone left, I brought out my surprise—cherry red Marucci baseball bats for every single member of the team. I'd ordered a hundred of them, custom made by Marucci, the same Louisiana company that had made those for the New Orleans Saints; only this time, they were inscribed with a slightly different message:

SCALISE WHIP TEAM 2014
BRING THE WOOD

The place went wild. The bats were a hit! And I felt they were a way of proving that even if we were underdogs, we were a team. And we had style.

✤ ✤ ✤

The next morning, I was just about as anxious as I've ever been in my life. Jen and the kids had flown up for the vote. Maddie and Harrison stayed in my office while Jen went ahead to the committee room, where the vote would take place.

Speeches had to be made, votes cast, votes counted. It felt like forever, and as I sat there, Jen's hand in mine, I tried to push from my mind the possibility, or even probability, that I wouldn't make the runoff.

As my mind spiraled, Cathy McMorris Rodgers, the conference chair, took the podium to give the results.

"I'm proud to announce that our new whip," she began—*our new whip*; that meant no runoff, that meant one of us managed to get enough votes in just one round—"is Steve Scalise."

My eyes filled with tears. Before I even really registered what had happened I felt Jen's hand squeezing mine, and when I looked at her, she had tears in her eyes too, and suddenly we were both crying, all the emotion and exhaustion of that whole crazy two-week sprint flooded from me. After that, it was a whirlwind. An impromptu acceptance speech, a press conference, all the while trying to slip away so I could find my kids. They were heading from my office toward me, and when I finally slipped away and ran down into the tunnels under the buildings, we saw each other, my kids and I, running toward each other from opposite directions, and we all went nuts. They couldn't completely understand what all the fuss was about; they just saw how happy their father was, and that's all they needed. They jumped up into my arms. We hugged, celebrated, and cried while a New Orleans TV crew caught us in all our giddiness and euphoria, immortalizing one of the happiest moments of my life.

✣ ✣ ✣

The next day, the sergeant at arms stopped by my office.

"Sir," he said, "congratulations on your win. Now that

you're going to be whip, we need to talk about your security detail."

My what?

I hadn't even thought of that.

In all the craziness of the previous days, I'd had no time to think about it. But of course. Because of this almost impossible series of events—an unprecedented political upset, an insanely fast campaign, an unexpected, underdog victory—I was now a member of leadership.

Being in leadership meant I'd be assigned armed officers of the Capitol Police Dignitary Protection Division, who would divide into teams and be with me all day, every day, wherever I went.

To be honest, it felt a little over the top.

6:20 AM

THE DIGNITARY PROTECTION DIVISION

About 20 feet from the entrance to the baseball field, on the first base side, Special Agent Crystal Griner and Special Agent David Bailey sat in a Suburban with the windows down, the radio on low, chatting and keeping an eye on the area, when a gunman walked up to what otherwise would have been a completely defenseless team of congressmen and senators.

Three years into my life with a security detail, I'd finally grown used to their near-constant presence. Back home all my old friends still ragged on me when I walked into a restaurant with a few extra men and women in suits. "Steve, what do *you* need Secret Service for?"

If you're a member of the Capitol Police Dignitary Protection Division, it's an occupational hazard that you get mistaken for Secret Service. Most of them don't mind. Or at least, they pretend not to mind. Or at least they *used* to pretend not to mind, until the Secret Service got into some trouble a few years ago. Now Dignitary Protection Division agents politely point out the difference.

I'd grown close to the men and women in my detail. It was awkward and intrusive at first, but then eventually, they began to feel like family. They seemed to view me less as a target to protect and more as a friend, even family member, which is how I viewed them. They sought to keep me not just safe but also comfortable. They're deliberate about trying not to crowd me, but they're always nearby, always watching, monitoring the crowds, looking for exits, ready to act.

Jennifer and the kids have grown close to the detail, too, although the kids have always been a little uncomfortable with the idea that I need one. When I leave the house with them, my daughter asks my wife, "Remind me again why Daddy needs his detail?"

It's hard to accept that your father might be a target, even in a completely hypothetical scenario we assure them would never happen. The agents try to make it easier on the kids, Dave and Crystal especially. They're both gentle and extraordinarily kind. Both athletes—Dave was a football player in school, a defensive back, and Crystal played college basketball—they can look so focused that they seem unapproachable, but then you speak with them and realize how thoughtful and caring they are. Dave joined the Capitol Police because he wanted to protect people. Really, because he wanted to *help* people. You'd never guess from looking at him, a man in a well-tailored suit with a plastic earpiece and a pistol on his hip, but he was a teacher first. He might have been a teacher his whole life, but he wanted to buy his mother a house and couldn't see a way of making that happen fast enough on his teacher's salary. So he decided to help people another way. If you spent time around either Dave or Crystal, you'd almost worry they're too nice to have what it takes if something goes down.

Almost.

✢ ✢ ✢

Over on the third base line, a shot rang out, and a bullet raced toward Trent Kelly's head at a few thousand feet per second.

The round clipped a link in the fence, knocking it off its trajectory just enough that it went just wide of Kelly's head, instead of right into it, as the sound echoed across the park.

Over in the Suburban, Dave and Crystal looked at each other.

Dave thought a car had backfired.

Out on the field, there was a moment of suspension.

It was still a beautiful day, still a bunch of guys having fun, still a baseball practice, just one with a loud noise.

Then the gunman aimed at me.

Dave and Crystal heard the second bang.

They looked at each other again. "Okay, that's definitely a gunshot."

Dave jumped out of the car. The echo was so loud he thought someone was shooting from behind him. He looked around, scanned his surroundings, trying to identify the source of the sound, but he was now looking in exactly the wrong direction.

After the gunman fired at me, he moved the barrel to the right and fired again, hitting Matt Mika, a lobbyist for Tyson's Foods, in the chest. The bullet passed millimeters from Mika's heart, which was now visible from the outside, through a sucking chest wound.

He shot Mika again, through his left arm, severing a nerve.

Mika was down.

The gunman panned to the outfield and shot at Zach Barth, a 24-year-old staffer who started running toward the outfield fence, but when he got there, he found no exit, no gate to open; he was trapped. With the gunman firing at him, Zach dove to the ground, but he felt bullets hitting the earth around him, getting closer, until he felt one hit him in the leg.

Another staffer ran toward Rand Paul, who was on the other side of the fence; Paul saw the staffer vault himself up and over a 20-foot section of fence in what seemed like a second or two. The two of them tried to find a tree to hide behind, but since no one knew where the gunman was, they didn't know what they were hiding from.

Over by the Suburban, Dave heard the other shots, and now he knew he was looking in the wrong direction. He turned back toward the front of the car and saw everyone running away from the field. He knew they must be running away from the danger.

So he ran toward it.

He had only a vague idea where the gunfire was coming from, but he saw me take the last of my steps and collapse.

The sides closed in. Dave had tunnel vision. He wasn't responding like he was trained to protect me; he was responding like he was *created* to protect me, like he was specially wired that way. He ran for me, but he'd taken only a few steps toward me when a bullet flashed in front of him. He could feel it; he felt like he could almost *see* it, a massive bullet moving at high velocity, passing millimeters from his face. It snapped him out of the zone, his field of vision widened again, and, for the first time, he saw the gunman.

Dave pulled out his gun and started firing.

He was standing in the open, out on the field, but he wasn't thinking about the fact that he had no cover. He had no bulletproof vest on under his suit that day, and it wouldn't have mattered; it wouldn't have stopped a bullet that big moving that fast and, if anything, probably would have made it worse.

A high-velocity bullet that size likely would have gone right through the vest, pulling Kevlar into his body.

Dave knew all that but pushed it from his mind. He wasn't even really thinking about the man he was shooting at. All he was trying to do—his entire reason for existing at that moment—was to draw danger toward himself. He was trying to take the focus off me and my colleagues.

The gunman aimed at Dave and fired a shot right on target.

The bullet hit the iPhone clipped to Dave's waist, which shattered, and probably saved him from a devastating wound like mine.

He didn't even notice. He was totally focused on making his shots count. He only had one magazine with him, the one in his gun, and he knew he had to make it matter each time he pulled the trigger. He couldn't go squeezing off rounds rapid-fire; he didn't have enough ammo. And he'd registered that he was surrounded by civilians. He was aware, without having to look, of a coffee shop behind him, a YMCA in front of him, people he'd seen moments before walking dogs and taking kids to school all around him. He'd taken all of this in, registered it, processed it, and funneled it into awareness he could maintain without really thinking about it.

Even as he stood on the field, out in the open, with a gunman squeezing off high-velocity rounds rapid-fire from a high-capacity magazine at him, Dave forced himself to slow down.

Aim, breathe, fire. Aim, breathe, fire. Like it was just him on a quiet day at the range.

The gunman was, for the moment, pinned down, engaged with Dave in a firefight across the baseball diamond, and Dave knew that was good, the team was safe for the moment, but it was an unfair fight. Dave managed to get 10 shots off with his service pistol. The gunman fired a dozen from his high-powered semi-automatic rifle, then two dozen; within seconds he'd fired more than 30 rounds; then, in a flash, more than 60. Dave didn't stand a chance against that kind of firepower, but as long as Dave and the gunman were shooting at each other, the players were safe. Dave had no problem being in danger, just as long as no one else was.

In the outfield, Zach Barth, still pressed to the ground trying to hide, saw his chance to make a run for it, with the gunman now occupied in a firefight across the diamond. He got up and made an adrenaline-fueled sprint for cover, ignoring the hole in his leg, charging toward the dugout where other members were huddled for cover, arriving with a literal leap into the arms of his boss, Coach Roger Williams.

Now it was a race against the clock. Most of us were trapped. The only hope for those crouching in the dugout was that somehow the gunman hadn't noticed them there.

Then a shot rang out, and a bullet crashed into the dugout's cinderblock wall.

If there'd been any doubt whether the gunman knew players were hiding in the dugout, there wasn't anymore. He'd seen them. He'd fired at them. He'd get to them soon, and they'd have nowhere to go. The players there were unarmed, confined to a small space. They were sitting ducks. The gunman would be able to mow them all down, to kill a dozen congressmen in a matter of seconds, plus staffers and other volunteers. It'd easily be the worst political assassination in the country's history. He just needed to get onto the field. He just needed to take a few steps toward them, just get a *slightly* better angle.

Dave wasn't letting him do that. As long as Dave was standing out there firing from his pistol, the gunman was pinned down.

But Dave could feel his gun getting light.

He hadn't been counting rounds, but he knew he had to be close to empty. He had to leave the field. He had no choice. He needed more ammo; he had no more on him, but there were a few extra magazines in the trunk of the SUV.

Dave took off running toward the Suburban.

✣ ✣ ✣

Back in the Suburban, Special Agent Griner couldn't see the gunman.

When Dave ran out onto the field, Griner got on the radio to call for help, but there were two problems.

First, she was still on the driver's side, where it seemed like the open door might provide some cover toward the field, but the gunman wasn't on the field. He'd started moving closer to her, toward her blindside. Dave had forced him to change his plans. The gunman now knew that to get to the congressmen huddled in the dugout, he had to go through Dave and Crystal. So he'd set out to kill Dave and Crystal. And Crystal still didn't know where he was.

As the gunman crept south on the other side of the field, along the fence that runs along the third baseline, moving toward home plate, toward the backstop, he'd soon have a clear, unobstructed shot at Crystal. She had the car door providing some cover, but only from the north. The threat was from the west. It was from her left flank, which was totally exposed.

The other problem was that the radio in the Suburban was tuned to Capitol Police dispatch, which was all the way on the southern side of the Capitol, seven miles way, across the river. There was no way they'd be able to get there anytime soon. The Capitol Police is able to coordinate directly with the Park Police, though, and the Park Police has Medevac helicopters.

By 7:09 AM, neighbors had started making 911 calls, which were routed to the Department of Emergency Communications, and then, from there, to the Alexandria Police Department. The first transmissions out to the officers on patrol were incongruously tame—"reports of a weapons violation." Then the trickle of 911 calls became a flood. Calls began coming in so quickly that the lines jammed, callers couldn't get through, and people started finding other ways to get help. One woman walked right up to a nearby fire station and simply rang the doorbell. Five squad cars were dispatched at first, but within minutes, the police department upgraded the call to "all available units report." All over the city, officers turned on their lights and sirens, ambulance teams from two nearby fire stations mobilized, and an emergency response team from Reagan National Airport ran out to their vehicle and took off toward the baseball field.

The cavalry was coming.

But rush hour had started, traffic for many of the responders was bumper to bumper, and the only people on-site capable of shooting back were the two members of my security detail.

And they were running out of ammo.

✜ ✜ ✜

Crystal still couldn't see the gunman, but he was moving closer and closer to her, from her blind side. Dave had funneled the gunman away from us but toward his partner. As Dave ran back to the car, he saw what was about to happen. *"CRYS-TAL!"* he screamed. *"GET ON THE OTHER SIDE!"*

But even as he tried to warn her, Crystal was already moving—she'd just seen some of the players dragging Matt Mika toward the parking lot. He had been next to me, near first base, when he was shot through the chest and the arm. Though Griner couldn't see exactly what had happened to Mika, she sensed it was bad and wanted to get to him, to do whatever she could to help. Everything was happening at once. Crystal was trying to help a wounded player, Dave was running back to the Suburban, and as Crystal moved, she saw, for the first time, the gunman across the lot behind home plate.

She saw him emerge from the storage shed, aim the SKS at the Suburban, and fire.

Crystal knew instinctively what she needed to do. She didn't even have to talk to Dave; the two of them were in sync. She stepped out from behind the vehicle, out into the open, drawing the threat to herself just as Dave had in the field a moment ago, giving her partner a moment of cover. One shot, two shots toward the storage shed. Three, four. She was out-gunned, but for the moment, that was okay; she knew she just had to give Dave a few seconds.

With Crystal occupying the gunman, Dave ran to the trunk of the Suburban, yanked it open, grabbed the book bag from the back, and crouched against the vehicle, digging around for the two mag pouches he had stashed in the bag. He loaded one into the pistol grip, stood up, and rejoined the fight.

Bullets were flying everywhere now, going through windows of storefronts and vehicles, flying above the pool over at the YMCA, knocking over bicycles, and perforating the Suburban. Glass smashed, paneling crumpled, air hissed out of tires. Both sides had their cover. My security detail was firing from the Suburban. Dave was braced over the hood, and he could *feel* the bullets hitting the vehicle. The ones smashing the windshield were inches from his face; they felt like explosions he was impossibly close to, almost inside of.

The gunman disappeared for a few seconds, then reappeared, firing from the other side of the storage shed. Crystal and Dave both ran to the back of the car to try and return fire from there.

The gunman disappeared again, and reemerged where he'd been the first time.

Crystal and Dave ran to the front of vehicle, and bent over the engine block again.

Each time they switched positions, they had to run around Mika, who was lying by the back tire, bleeding. Crystal knew he was still alive; Dave thought he was dead, because he was covered in blood and wasn't moving.

When the gunman popped out on the north side of the storage shed one more time, Crystal stepped out to return fire, but again, she had no cover; when she and Dave were firing from near the front of the car, they could lean over the engine block, but from the back, she just had to step out beyond the car, into the open. It was an extraordinary risk, especially because the gunman was firing higher velocity bullets from a weapon with an effective range that was four times longer than hers and, relative to Crystal, he had effectively unlimited ammunition.

Crystal knew she was exposed and at tremendous risk, but her instinct was similar to Dave's, that it was okay to be in harm's way, just as long as she was drawing the danger away from the field, where the players were crouching for cover. She was trained for this, as much as anyone can be trained for something that had never happened before. These agents were acting partly because they're always prepared, but partly just out of pure courage, a kind of courage and heroism I still can't quite grasp. I still can't quite understand where it came from.

Crystal stepped out from behind the vehicle one more time to return fire, another *crack* echoed from behind the storage shed, and Dave saw his partner drop.

✤ ✤ ✤

Dave heard Crystal gasp, and yell, "I'm hit."

The bullet shattered her ankle. She struggled to get back up to her feet, but her leg gave out. She put her pistol to the ground to try and push herself back up, but her leg couldn't support any weight. She couldn't stand.

Dave stopped shooting and ran to help his partner. He ran through a series of thoughts and emotions—relieved it was just an ankle, devastated it'd been her rather than him who'd taken the bullet, worried that she was still in the line of fire. He helped pull her behind the wheel well, which, other than the engine block, provided the most solid cover, put the most metal between her and the gunman. Then he moved back and started looking for the gunman again, while yelling to his fallen partner, "Hold on, Crystal. Hold on!" Trying to find the gunman, trying to comfort his partner.

Crystal didn't need comforting; she was still trying to figure out how to rejoin the fight. From behind the wheel well, her ankle crushed and bleeding, she repositioned herself so she could aim under the vehicle, using the space between the pavement and the chassis like an arrow slit. She couldn't quite get an angle though; it was too narrow, trying to go beneath the vehicle, across a hundred feet of asphalt, at a fleeting target ducking back and forth from behind a wall of concrete.

The gunman kept firing; more rounds struck the car.

Unable to get quality shots off, Crystal shifted her attention to Mika. She moved herself toward him and put her body over his, creating a human shield so any bullets that came their way would hit her, not him. She spoke to him, trying to keep him engaged and awake.

With Crystal down, the advantage shifted decisively in the gunman's favor. It was one-on-one again, Dave and his service pistol against an assailant with good cover, a more powerful weapon, a pistol he hadn't even used yet, and way more ammunition.

A bullet hit the pavement near Dave and fragmented, the shrapnel flying into his leg. His shoe started filling up with blood.

Back behind the storage shed, the gunman withdrew for a moment. He popped out the spent magazine and let it clatter to the pavement. He took out a fully loaded 40-round banana clip, stuck it in the rifle, charged his weapon, stepped out from behind the shed, and started shooting at Dave.

Dave, meanwhile, was on his last magazine.

He knew that as long as he kept firing, the gunman would stay pinned down, stuck behind that shed, unable to walk out into the field to finish the slaughter. But Dave was about to run out of ammo. Already outgunned, he would soon become effectively weaponless. Crystal was down and unable to engage.

The gunman would soon have free rein.

In the dugout, the moment of hope was beginning to dwindle. The only weapon anyone had was a baseball bat. Once the gunman was no longer pinned down, which was only a few seconds away, we'd all be sitting ducks.

Dave anchored himself to the ground next to the side-view mirror, bent over the front of the Suburban, and tried to make his last shots count.

The gunman just had to wait a little more, draw a few more rounds at the storage shed, and then he'd be able to finish his massacre.

Dave tried to stay calm. But just as he was reaching the last of his ammo, he heard another gunman.

And this one was behind him.

Dave was surrounded.

6:56 AM

Ten more minutes. I'd be ready to leave in 10 minutes.

It was like being a kid out on the sandlot. Then a world-shattering tragedy: Mom calling out that dinner's ready. *Ten more minutes, Mom! Fifteen, tops!*

I had a reason for staying as long as I could: This was the last practice. The game was tomorrow. My family was coming up, and the game was at Nationals Park, the new 41,000-seat stadium. Sure, we wouldn't exactly be packing the stands, but we'd have a few thousand people there and, most importantly, my wife and kids wearing their GEAUX SCALISE shirts.

There was a little added pressure this year, too. The score between Democrats and Republicans, going back to the first game in 1909, was tied. Republicans had won 39 times. Democrats had won 39 times. This was our chance to pull ahead in the series. Not to mention I *knew* Cedric Richmond, one of my best friends in Congress and the star player for the Democrats, was going to be at the top of his game. I couldn't let him have another win. I needed to be ready. I needed to squeeze as much out of the last practice as I could.

By then it had turned into a bright, clear day, and I decided a few more minutes wouldn't throw my schedule off too much.

I take practice seriously. I attend every single one. I have fun on the field, but in my mind, I'm at the game. When I take my turn at batting practice, I'm pretending the batting practice pitcher is Cedric. I'm making him work the strike zone. I'll let a dozen balls zing past without swinging if I don't think they're strikes, while the other players roll their eyes. "Swing or give someone else a chance, Scalise!" I'm not a power guy, I'm not hitting home runs; I'm all about getting on base, singles and doubles and drawing walks, so a good eye for balls and strikes is key. Batting practice for me is as much about honing my eye for the strike zone as it is actually hitting the ball. And when I'm out in the field, I'm scooping every grounder like the Democrats are about to score the winning run.

So that's what I was doing at that practice, just sitting there in position at second base, thinking of excuses to stay longer, like I was in high school, just like the pick-up football and basketball and softball games after the last bell rang at Archbishop Rummel High, me and the guys squeezing as much fun out of the day before the sun goes down. I was in the zone. *We* were in the zone. We'd been playing well. We were almost ready.

I should have left to get ready for the day, go over my remarks for the red snapper announcement, and prepare for my other meetings, but I felt too good. I knew the red snapper talking points backward and forward, so why not stay out a little longer? The sun felt good. The sound of bats hitting leather was like music. My arm felt good, tensile, and I'll grant you, the throw from second to first isn't a country mile, but I felt I could fire that thing over the Potomac if I needed to. I had that coiled energy. It was just a good day, a good practice, and as Congressman Duncan walked off the field and fist bumped me, I thought, *Yeah, we're ready; we're loose, but we're focused.*

✛ ✛ ✛

All the grounders are coming to middle infield, and I am scooping them up and firing them over to first base without bobbling even one of them, just hoovering them up, firing them over, running and scooping and firing, one after the other. I am in my rhythm, in the zone, scooping and throwing, scooping and throwing, my body feeling good, my 51-year-old frame feeling lithe and elastic. Suddenly I notice how the last hint of that faint morning chill has cooked off to make way for a pure, early summer heat, and then there is a bang. I think, *That's okay; it's nothing.* I'm still standing there in the sun thinking about strategy and Cedric's fastball and my family and my son's first U2 concert and a tractor—I see a tractor and the noise makes sense, except there's no one on the tractor. There's another noise, and I can't force it out anymore; I have to allow this new reality to press itself in on me, that someone is shooting.

It's strange though; gunfire and baseball don't fit together, and it's also strange that there's a kind of numbness around my waist. A kind of pressure, like a lineman has lowered his shoulder and given me a shove.

But it's not a shove. It's a large 7.62 caliber bullet moving at high velocity that has entered my hip and hit my femur, and my leg has effectively detonated. The bones explode. My femur explodes, my pelvis explodes; a puff of bone and metal fragments fly through my pelvis and abdominal cavity, turning my body into a shrapnel-packed bomb going off in a confined space. The support structure that keeps the whole architecture of my body upright is now a broken-apart puzzle, and there's no exit wound, so there's nowhere for all that energy to go. Hard things ricochet around like pinballs, severing veins and slicing open organs, shredding through my intestines and destroying my digestive tract, rattling nerves, making everything bleed all at once.

But all the damage is internal. Except for one almost imperceptibly small hole in my baseball pants, it's invisible from the outside.

I'm trying to move on pulverized leg bones.

I feel like someone else is controlling my legs.

My legs stop working. It's not pain exactly, and I don't know that the reason I'm falling is because my whole foundation has imploded. I feel instead like the wiring that connects my brain to my legs has been unplugged.

I fall.

Now I'm on my hands in the dirt, facing the outfield.

I don't know why I'm facing the outfield, when I was just facing the other way.

I don't know that the force with which the bullet hit me has spun me almost all the way around.

Things I don't know are replaced by things I do know. The shooting hasn't stopped; I know that. I can hear more and more gunfire.

I know that to survive I have to run away from it.

I know I can't run away from it because I can't move my legs.

I have to crawl.

Somehow I know that the gunman is behind me. Something tells me that. Some invisible system in my body has run a kind of algebra, an algorithm that's taken information in, run the numbers, and calculated, without me even being conscious of it that because my body spun to where it is, and because the bullet entered where it did, the bullet must have come from the infield. So now I'm moving away from the infield as fast as I can.

Which is not very fast at all.

One arm after the other, barely making progress. Bullets cracking overhead. An army crawl, but without legs. I'm trying to swim on dry land.

I dig my palms into the dirt so hard that pebbles implant in my palms, almost totally buried in the skin. I pull, and pull, and pull. I claw at that dense, red clay. I move inches at a time. Safety seems impossibly far away, unreachable. More bullets zing above me. I pull for 10 minutes but it feels like a half hour, an hour. I know I'm going to lose my arms soon, just like I lost my legs. The ground becomes softer.

I've reached the grass. I somehow notice, despite everything going on, that the grass is still damp with dew. It feels like a year ago that I lost my legs. It's starting to happen again with my arms, a fuzzy cellphone connection that I'm losing, my conversation partner disappearing into a tunnel. I need to keep moving away from the shots before I lose control of my arms. But each pull becomes harder and harder.

There's a word for what's happening to me: *exsanguination.* My body is emptying itself of blood. I'm bleeding so much that I will die. I'm painting the field with a two-foot-wide brush stroke of blood, but mixed in with the grass it doesn't look so much like blood. It's not really red but brown, like the grass decided to die as I moved past.

The gunfire hasn't stopped. Someone is still coming after me.

But strangely, it isn't fear that's overtaking me. It's just a very clear goal. I have to get away from the gunfire. I'm inching away from it, and at any moment, whoever's shooting might walk up to me, casual as you like, and execute me on the ground. I feel like all that's stopping him is that I'm escaping. At an excruciatingly slow pace.

Then it happens. I lose control of my arms. I can't move them, I can't make them do anything at all, and I know what I need to do.

With my face in the dirt, grass and dew filling my nostrils, I begin to pray.

And as I do, I see clearly big church doors opening, and I see, framed there like an angel, a young woman. I feel I recognize her. I know her. She's mine. It's my daughter, Madison; it's the grown-up version of my 10-year-old daughter, 15 or 20 years in the future, standing in a wedding dress, framed by those big doors. She's alone. There's no one next to her. No one's there to walk her down the aisle, because she has no father. Because I'm not there for her.

I feel a twist in my gut, and now I know what I need to pray for. *Please God,* I pray, *don't let Madison walk down the aisle alone. Please, she's daddy's little girl. Let me be there. Please, just let me be there with her. Please God, let me see my family again; let me see Jen and the kids again.*

The shooting changes.

It doesn't stop. In fact, it seems to increase. But it becomes a different kind of sound. I can tell that it's coming from somewhere new. A different sound means a different caliber. I know what that means.

It means we're shooting back.

We're shooting back. The realization comes over me as a relief. *Dave and Crystal are shooting back.*

Please God, protect Dave and Crystal. Let their aim be true. Let them carry out their mission. I realize I feel calm now. That, actually, I've felt that way since the moment I started to pray, a powerful sense of calm coming over me.

I think of more things to ask for, so I ask for those too.

I'm being a little more demanding than I usually am when I pray—less a servant of His will and more like a child focusing intently on a Christmas list, but it centers me. I can feel a burden being lifted off of me. I feel a weight disappearing. Like someone is saying, *Okay, a bad thing is happening; you're hit, but I'm just gonna take some of that burden away from you.* A calm voice saying, *Hang in there, Steve,* with a slight Southern twang, *We're gonna get ya.* It sounds so real, it can't just be in my mind, and before I can think, *Huh, so God has a Southern twang,* I hear it again.

I'm watching, Steve. We haven't forgotten ya. We're gonna get ya.

And I realize, I *do* recognize that voice. That's Mike Conaway, our first basemen and the congressman from Texas's 11th district. When my arms gave out and everything started powering down, my head was turned toward first base, so once I understand I'm hearing Mike's voice, I understand I can see him over there, too. He's not too far away. He's calling to me, comforting me.

And I know I'm not alone.

7:12 AM

THE POLICE

At about that time a 16-year veteran of the Alexandria Police Department named Kevin Jobe had just come on duty and was attending morning roll call. By a quarter to seven, he was out in a cruiser.

The police station is over three miles from the field, but his patrol took him east, past the old Masonic national memorial that sits atop Shooters Hill. It took him in the direction of the Potomac, Eugene Simpson Stadium Park, and City Hall.

He made it as far as North Patrick and Madison Street, in Alexandria's scenic Old Town, before he heard a call go over police dispatch: Something was happening at the baseball field, an incident with an active shooter.

Around the time Officer Jobe was coming on duty, one of his colleagues, a young officer named Alexander Jensen, who had only two years with the Alexandria Police Department under his belt, was supposed to be getting off his shift. Jensen had been on duty since 8:30 PM the night before.

Just before his shift ended that morning, Jensen stopped in front of Cora Kelly Elementary School, less than two miles from where I lay, to help keep an eye on the morning school traffic, as buses and parents drove up to drop off students.

✤ ✤ ✤

Officer Jobe's route had taken him within a few thousand feet of the field when the "active shooter" call came over the radio. He pulled north onto North Patrick Street, which becomes Route 1 and which is, with two lanes in each direction, the fastest way to the park.

He was able to make it to the park in under three minutes.

As he pulled up, it was quickly clear that this wasn't any kind of false alarm: People were sprinting, trying to get away as fast as they could, but there wasn't any order to it; it wasn't clear what they were running from. Officer Jobe called to them through the car window to them, trying to get some kind of guidance. A few of them pointed toward one of the baseball fields, and at the exact moment they pointed, a volley of *cracks* sounded from somewhere near the YMCA, all the way on the other side of the park from him. It seemed like it might be coming from some-place hidden by the trees. Jobe couldn't be sure. But it was obvi-ous the sound was coming from a high-powered weapon.

He knew that in order to help, he had to get closer. It'd be suicide to move in without knowing where the shooting was coming from, especially when, for all he knew, there were shooters who could see him. He decided to continue on foot. He wouldn't be protected, but he'd be harder to spot. He parked the car by the soccer field, got out, drew his service pistol, and started moving toward the sound of gunfire.

He passed the soccer field, and then the baseball field next to the one we were on, then a basketball court that sits along the first baseline. More bystanders yelled to Jobe, "He's behind the shed!"

Jobe still couldn't see the gunman, but he heard another

volley of gunfire. He skipped down a small hill toward a parking lot, and that's when the whole scene opened up to him. A black SUV was parked in front of him, and by the front of the car, Jobe saw a man in plainclothes shooting toward a blue storage shed, using the hood of the car for cover.

Jobe had just come up on David Bailey.

He was behind Dave, off his right shoulder, and Dave, totally focused on that blue shed, didn't notice the Alexandria police officer moving in behind him.

Jobe, for his part, had no way of knowing just how much ammunition the gunman had and didn't know that, until that very moment, the man braced over the hood of the Suburban was all that stood between the gunman and the worst political massacre in American history. Jobe had no way of knowing that Dave was on his last magazine, about to run out of ammo, or that Crystal, Dave's only other backup, was down.

Jobe had arrived with nearly miraculous speed, and still, he was there at the very last possible moment.

✤ ✤ ✤

Alexander Jensen had been finishing up his shift in front of the school when the "shots fired" call came over dispatch. Even though he was just minutes away from going home after his all-night shift, he put the car in gear and turned his lights and sirens on. He pulled out onto Commonwealth Avenue, which runs toward the park, and stepped on the gas.

Just as he approached the first intersection, another car came careening into a view. It was another police cruiser—this was Officer Nicole Battaglia, another young officer in the Alexandria Police Department, just 18 months on the job, also responding to the call.

Jensen let her pull in front, and then the two raced south toward the field, both turning onto East Monroe, which put them just a few blocks from the park.

The field came into view. Both of them were heading right to the gunman.

Neither could see him.

✜ ✜ ✜

From his position behind Dave and Crystal, Officer Jobe saw the two police cruisers come racing in down East Monroe Avenue, and he could see what was about to happen. Whichever officers were in those cars, they were about to put themselves right in front of the gunman, and from the speed with which they were approaching, it seemed like they didn't see him. Jobe grabbed his radio. "Alexandria units! Stop where you are!"

A second later, both of the cars flying down the avenue screeched to a halt.

Jensen's location, when he heard Officer Jobe's warning, was just 200 feet from the gunman. Nicole Battaglia was a little up the road from him.

Jensen still couldn't see the gunman, but he was close enough to hear the roar of the rifle and to get a general sense of where it was coming from. He used his cruiser to block the entrance to the YMCA, so no one would stumble onto the scene and get struck in the line of fire; then he got out and took cover behind the car, scanning the scene, until finally he saw the gunman.

The man stood in front of the blue shed with what looked like an AK-47, the butt stock right up against his shoulder. Jensen clicked his radio and relayed what he was seeing. He was a second too late.

Just up ahead of him, Officer Battaglia still didn't know where the gunman was, but she'd gotten out of her car and was running toward the scene. The gunman could see her clearly. He aimed at the young officer running toward him, barely 100 feet from him and getting closer, still not seeing him.

To the southwest, behind his cruiser, Jensen heard a half dozen rapid-fire shots.

To the east, Officer Jobe heard it too.

Just in front of Jobe, Dave Bailey saw the young officer emerge and move toward the gunman; then he heard the burst and saw her fall from view.

✢ ✢ ✢

Nicole Battaglia was impossibly close to the gunman by the time she saw a rifle barrel pointed in her direction. She tried to dive behind a car just as he opened fire.

A moment later, her voice came over the radio.

"I'm taking fire!"

She'd managed to roll behind a Lexus just as the bullets came at her; somehow all of them missed her, half of them smashing into the side of the car. She was okay, and she'd given Jensen, who was still behind his cruiser, a momentary advantage; the gunman's attention was elsewhere.

Jensen moved quickly. He ran to the trunk and took out the Bushmaster rifle, and then went back and braced himself over the hood of the car, using it to steady his aim. The gunman was 200 feet away—Jensen could make that shot. He looked past the gunman to see if there were any civilians downrange. He had a momentary window, a clean shot. He aimed and pulled the trigger.

The rifle didn't fire.

Jensen ducked behind the wheel well again—the firing chamber was empty.

Of course.

The rifle was in "cruiser safe" mode; you don't keep it loaded and charged in the trunk.

Jensen chambered a round, rose from behind the cruiser again, found the gunman, aimed, and pulled the trigger.

The Bushmaster recoiled, the gun cracked, but Jensen missed, and now he'd given away his position. The gunman turned toward him. Jensen ducked down behind the car again. Now he was pinned down. He knew the gunman would be fixing his aim right over the hood of the car, where Jensen's head had just been. If Jensen tried to rise back up to take another shot, he'd be easily picked off.

Jensen had an idea. He shimmied from the front of the cruiser to the back, so that when he popped up, he'd be in a different place and the gunman would have to sight him again.

When he rose to look over the trunk, he saw the gunman's attention was back on the Suburban.

Jensen aimed over the trunk, steadied himself, and pulled the trigger again.

Another crack, the rifle recoiled again, and over by the shed, the gunman stumbled. The rifle fell from his hands and clattered to the ground, just out of reach. The gunman pulled his pistol out of the holster and stood back up.

Jensen ducked down again and shimmied to the front of the cruiser.

✛ ✛ ✛

Over to the north, near the SUV, Jobe couldn't see what had happened on the other side of the shed. Dave and Crystal couldn't see it either. None of them knew a young police officer had fired two shots, managed to hit the gunman, and knocked the rifle out of his hands.

What they saw, from their vantage point, was the gunman reappearing from behind the shed, for some reason holding a pistol instead of the rifle.

Jobe saw his chance. As Dave steadied himself and tried to make his last bullets count, he heard a gunshot coming from behind him.

Dave dropped, got low, made himself small, and for a terrifying moment, thought he was surrounded, that the gunman had an accomplice who'd joined the fight just as Dave ran out of ammo.

But as Dave turned to follow the sound, what he saw was not an accomplice but Officer Kevin Jobe of the Alexandria Police Department, standing bolt upright in his firing stance, locked in, focused on the gunman.

Dave knew the cavalry had arrived.

✜ ✜ ✜

Now they were working together, an unspoken coordination falling over them, an impromptu team of people who'd never met coming together for one purpose. The gunman was facing two men to the north, Nicole Battaglia scrambled back to her feet and moved in from the south, and Alexander Jensen was locked in and watching over all of them with the Bushmaster from his cruiser to the west.

Officer Jobe yelled at the gunman to get down, get back, and when he didn't listen, but just kept coming at them with his pistol, trying to squeeze off more rounds, Jobe fired, one, two, four rounds at the gunman.

Dave used the diversion from this new partner he'd never met to make the last of his magazine count. As Officer Jobe engaged the gunman, Dave took a breath, aimed, and got another shot off, and this one found its mark—the round took the gunman across the midline and spun him almost entirely around, knocking him right back into Alexander Jensen's line of sight.

Jensen saw the gunman suddenly stumble out into the open. This was it. Jensen aimed and fired.

The gunman fell again, shot through the other hip, the pistol clattering out of his hand, and as the gunman fell, Bailey and Jobe started to run toward him, with Battaglia moving in from the south, all of them converging on the gunman. He was still reaching for his pistol, but Jobe beat him to it, grabbed the gunman, cuffed him, and searched him for other weapons. In the gunman's pocket was an extra pistol clip, to go along with all his weapons and ammo scattered around him.

At 7:14 AM, Jobe took to the radio to tell everyone they had the gunman in custody.

The alert was relayed to other first responders and by people shouting all around the field, "Shooter down! Shooter down!"

✛ ✛ ✛

The whole series of events, from the moment the first person called 911 to the time Jobe had the gunman cuffed, took six minutes. When the Office of the Commonwealth's Attorney completed its compulsory "Use of Force Investigation and Analysis" to determine whether officers were justified in the use of deadly force, the attorney took the unusual step of including a kind of disclaimer: "The facts presented in this case are so clear-cut and so obviously required the agents and officers to use deadly force," it said, "that one might question why my office even conducted this review."

Still, by the time he was detained, the gunman had fired the better part of a hundred rounds—including the bullet that had entered my leg, hit my femur, and exploded.

That one small entry wound belied a massive, mostly internal hemorrhage that was about to kill me. I'd be dead in a matter of minutes, unless someone with some kind of x-ray vision happened to show up and was somehow able to see all the bleeding that couldn't be seen. I needed a miracle.

7:14 AM

US ARMY RESERVE
MAJOR BRAD ROBERT WENSTRUP

**344th Combat Support Hospital, 26 klicks west of
Baghdad City**

Just west of Baghdad City, Iraq, is a prison called Abu Ghraib.
The place became famous in the spring of 2004, when reve-
lations of prisoner abuse surfaced. The name "Abu Ghraib"
became synonymous with the worst features of the US invasion of Iraq.

Abu Ghraib also housed a combat support hospital, however, that represented the very best.

Inside, the year after those abuses, US Army Reserve
Major Brad Wenstrup slept in Cell Block D by night and, by
day, worked with a team of doctors and nurses in a mobile
hospital set up inside of a rundown garage. They worked to
save the lives and limbs not just of American servicemen and
-women, but Iraqis too. And not just Iraqi civilians, but even
Iraqi insurgents. Insurgent groups had little capacity for medical care. The enemy wasn't treating the enemy, so we did.
Major Wenstrup went to Iraq to serve as a representative of
the US military, but perhaps even more than that, to serve
as a representative of the medical community. And perhaps
even more than *that*, to serve as a human being. He believed it
wasn't his job as a doctor, or a Christian, to judge the alleged
transgressions of the wounded people brought before him. He

believed his duty was to help fix broken bodies. Judgment was for others, or for a higher power. He tried not to expend much energy identifying his patients or trying to find out what kind of people they were. So when he treated a man one day for an ulcer associated with diabetes, he didn't notice that the face matched one of the cards in the "Most Wanted" deck the US military handed out to servicemen and -women to help them identify senior members of Saddam Hussein's regime. His interpreter grumbled after the operation, "Do you know who that is?"

Wenstrup said he didn't.

"I hate that man," the interpreter said. "That's Chemical Ali."

Wenstrup was treating Saddam's first cousin, a man who oversaw mass killings and the use of chemical weapons against his own people.

It would make sense for it to have been people like Chemical Ali who left the biggest impression on Wenstrup; that he would remember the celebrities most clearly. But that wasn't the case.

One of the patients he remembers most vividly was a marine who came in unconscious but stable and who was most remarkable for the fact that he came in with a curious lack of information. Often, patients would come in to the combat hospital after a preliminary operation out in the field, and there'd be some kind of information about the person—what was done, what was found: "There's eight sponges and three clamps in there." Sometimes field medics scribbled a soldier's vital signs right on the skin with a Sharpie.

In this case, there was nothing, except what the surgical

team was able to glean by looking at him. He had a blunt impact injury, most likely from an improvised explosive device going off somewhere near him. He wasn't bleeding.

Or, it didn't look like he was bleeding.

What was strange, though, is that the wound started weeping. Not *gushing*, not even bleeding, not like a vessel was cut and blood was pouring out, just oozing, slowly, through a suture.

Something wasn't right.

The marine's blood pressure started to drop.

The team—led by a general surgeon and an orthopedic surgeon, with Wenstrup as a third set of hands—decided they had to open the patient up to try and figure out what was going on. When they did, they found that despite the lack of a big entry wound, the blast had done devastating damage inside. The impact of the blast had torn up internal organs and cut through a major blood vessel.

It turned out the solider *was* bleeding, badly. But he was bleeding inside, and the only external sign came when his abdominal cavity filled with so much blood it needed a place to escape and started to leak through the stitches.

By the time they realized how much internal damage the man had suffered, his blood pressure had bottomed out. They tried to stanch the internal bleeding, but he was already dead.

Wenstrup was devastated. This became the patient who stayed with him, the one he wonders about, the loss that eats at him. That soldier was the one who, when Wenstrup thought of him, could start the "What if's" buzzing around

Wenstrup's mind. What made it so difficult for Wenstrup was that he believed he and the team could have saved that man. If only they'd known. If they'd known just a *little* sooner what had happened; if someone out in the field had known that the lack of a big entry wound doesn't necessarily mean a lack of major hemorrhaging; if someone had gotten him to the hospital just a little quicker; if someone just a little earlier had said, "Hey, we need to check for internal bleeding."

Wenstrup, of course, could not have known he'd have the chance to rewrite that story. To *be* that man in the field, giving other doctors in a hospital at least a fighting chance to save a life.

What he did know was that he could not shake the loss. It hit him and the other members of that medical team hard. Some wept over that soldier. They remembered the exact date they lost the man they might have saved.

But if that young soldier's death haunted Wenstrup and diminished (in only his own estimation) what was otherwise an exemplary tour of duty, it was also a loss from which one good thing came.

In a very real way, that young soldier's death saved my life.

✤ ✤ ✤

Major Wenstrup returned from Iraq to Ohio and was offered 90 days before he had to go back to work at his medical practice, but he figured, "What am I going to do for 90 days? Wander around the house and stare at the walls?" He felt the biggest risk to people like himself, coming back from seeing the kind of trauma he'd seen—or maybe the biggest risk to anyone, for that matter—was feeling unnecessary. Decamping to the suburbs to stare at the walls was just about the worst thing you could do, and yet so many veterans seemed to be doing just that. The notion held by friends and colleagues that the right thing to do was to take some pressure off himself, take some time off—it proved how dangerously uninformed even the most well-meaning people were about what those returning from war really needed.

Wenstrup realized, who better than he to educate them? He decided to give a talk at a nearby gym, with slides and everything, about what he'd seen in Iraq. He tried to help people in the community learn what it was really like to be around combat, and he talked about some of the soldiers— "the kids," as he called them—who he and other doctors managed to save. As well as the ones they hadn't.

Wenstrup mesmerized the audience with his stories of combat and the astounding medical interventions from the front lines, the heroes he served with, those who gave their lives. He spoke about leadership, and ethics, and American heroes, and a few days after that first speech, someone from the audience approached him.

"I heard that talk you gave. Are you going to give it again?"

He thought, *Why not?* Veterans Day was coming up, so he decided to do a Veterans Day event. Four hundred fifty people showed up.

He did another event.

Then another.

He decided to make it a charitable venture and charged

$15 at the door. Soon he was raising tens of thousands of dollars for Disabled American Veterans.

He did 20 talks, then 30, then 100. He'd go into surgery in the morning, put his army uniform on, go to a Kiwanis or Rotary Club or a church, give the talk, and head back to the office in time to see patients before the end of the day.

Perhaps inevitably, he started to hear, "You should really think about running for office." People from the local Republican Party started asking him to think about the upcoming race for mayor. He wouldn't have a shot at winning, they told him, so he needn't worry too much about a big career change. He'd be running against a popular incumbent, a Democrat in a 70% Democratic city, an African American in a 50% African-American city, and a member of what was essentially a Cincinnati political dynasty. The Republican Party just wanted to field a respectable opponent.

"You'll be lucky if you get 35% of the vote," they told him. "But how many people get asked to run for mayor of a major city in the United States of America?"

That got him. Why not? He threw his hat in the ring, prepared a concession speech, and challenged the shoe-in Democratic incumbent.

As early balloting came back, Brad found himself in a position he hadn't even considered: He was in the lead.

After the early balloting, he had 51% of the vote. He thought, *Uh oh—I might have to change the end of my speech.*

At 10:30 PM, with the count having been delayed by technical difficulties, he was still winning.

By the end of the night, he'd lost, but he'd pulled in 46% of the vote, outperforming expectations, surprising everyone, including himself, and leaving an impression on the people of Cincinnati.

Perhaps most of all, he left an impression on his opponent.

They'd both run clean campaigns, and the mayor had come to admire Major Wenstrup while running against him. Shortly after the election, the mayor called the man who'd very nearly unseated him and asked if he'd join the team. "You know, I got to know you," the mayor said, "and I have an opening on our Board of Health. Can you send me your résumé? I'd like to consider you."

So Major Wenstrup served under his former opponent and found that the position the mayor gave him was a useful perch from which to help people. It also gave him a new perspective on what was going on at the national level. As he spent more time working for the city's Public Health Department, he began to wonder how anyone could be even remotely effective at public health policy in the federal government, without having training in healthcare. How could you work in the healthcare field if you'd never seen a patient? And yet people in Washington, D.C. did.

For that matter, he saw people making military decisions, even though they'd never served.

He began to feel that if people making decisions actually had experience, the decisions would be better. So in 2012, with the confidence and experience from his near upset in the mayoral campaign, Wenstrup ran for the US House of Representatives.

This time, he won.

And yet he never stopped being a doctor. Or an Army Reservist. Just after he first arrived in Congress, Brad got a call from the Chief of Orthopedics at Walter Reed, the military's main hospital just outside D.C.

"Can you stay this weekend? We've got a lot of wounded coming in."

So he did. Brad Wenstrup, now a lieutenant colonel (since then he's been promoted again to colonel) and a newly minted representative from Ohio's second congressional district, went to the hospital and scrubbed in.

In the break room between cases, two OR technicians were talking to each other, and one turned to Brad.

"Did you hear?" he asked. "There's a congressman here today."

✠ ✠ ✠

Brad Wenstrup was on the baseball team and drove to practice almost every day.

Almost every day, he gave Rodney Davis, from Illinois' 13th District, a ride there, but never a ride back. Brad always had to leave early; he always had 8:00 AM meetings back at the Capitol.

On any other day, he'd have been well on his way back by the time the shooting started.

But not on June 14th.

On that day, his schedule had an unexpected opening. His morning cleared. As he drove to the field, he told Davis, "Actually, you know what? Today I can give you a ride back. I'm staying for the whole thing today."

Just after 7:00 AM, when, normally Brad would have been halfway up the George Washington Memorial Parkway back

to the Capitol, he decided to take some extra fielding practice. We usually went into the batting cage after taking our
turn at batting practice out on the field, but Brad didn't like
the cage. The machine was a little wild. As we got closer to
the game and began getting ready for Cedric's fastball, we
cranked the speed up. Brad wasn't especially excited about the
prospect of getting hit by the wild, cranked up machine, so
instead of extra batting practice, he grabbed his glove and ran
out toward the outfield.

Then he changed his mind.

He didn't know exactly why. Maybe because the outfield
was a little crowded; he probably wouldn't get the chance
for much fielding practice. He turned and went back to the
dugout, switched his fielding glove for batting gloves, and
headed, reluctantly, toward the erratic pitching machine. It
was a sudden change of heart that ended up putting him in an
ideal position for what was about to happen.

Just as he was stepping under the net into the batting
cage, Brad heard a bang.

He looked at Mark Johnson, a lobbyist for Toyota, who
was about to start feeding balls into the machine.

Is that what I think it is?

Another bang rang out, and at that point, it seemed as if
everything started happening at once.

Brad stepped back out of the cage and heard Trent Kelly
screaming, "He's got a gun!"

He saw me go down.

Brad hit the deck as bullets started to fly.

Soon he could see everybody running, but there was

nowhere to get off the field, no escape except for the one gate by first base. Brad saw me start to crawl, and he scanned the field to find the source of the shooting. As the gunman ripped off more rounds from the third base side, and sound waves cracked off the building around him, Brad had a strange memory, not of his own time in combat, but, of all things, a scene from *Saving Private Ryan*, when a team from Easy Company moving through a meadow sees an enemy personnel carrier start taking fire. *Who's doing the shooting? Who's doing the shooting!* He had the line from the movie ringing in his head. *Where are the good guys? Where are the bad guys?*

It took most of us a few key seconds to realize, and then to accept, that we were under attack, but Brad recognized immediately and went into a state of heightened focus. The gunfire was so loud, though, he had the same problem Dave and Crystal were having: The row of large buildings behind him threw the sound back, so it seemed as though the shooting was coming from all around, from multiple shooters, none of whom he could actually see, all concentrating their fire on the field. In Iraq, Brad's job when they came under fire wasn't to fight back, unless there was no other choice; there were Quick Reaction Forces for that. His mission was, the very first second it was safe to move, to get to the operating room. The moment you weren't pinned down, get to the hospital and get ready to help. So once he saw Dave go out into the field, see the gunman, and start firing back, Brad began thinking, *How quickly can I get there to help? What's the best way to help? Who's in the most need?*

His instinct was to keep his eyes on me, to not let me out of his sight. Even though it sounded like he might be surrounded by multiple shooters, Brad was actually in an ideal position. He and I were separated by a few layers of fencing, but we weren't very far from each other. He didn't have much cover from the gunman, but the crown of the field, the way it slopes down from the middle to the sides, and the layers of fencing along both baselines provided a visual screen. Because of his last-minute change of heart, his decision not to go out into the field, he was effectively invisible to the gunman.

Brad could tell now that at least one of the shooters was over by the third base line. He was still worried about more. He was worried about people trying to climb the fences to get away; they'd be exposed and easily picked off. But he understood that he himself was in the best position he could be.

Then Dave made his move back to the Suburban for more ammo, and the gunman moved with him, following along the third base line.

Brad realized he was about to be exposed.

Soon, the gunman and the security detail would be firing at each other from opposite sides of an open parking area next to the field.

Brad saw a rifle barrel emerge from behind a building near home plate.

At that moment, a passerby who'd dived behind a trashcan and started recording video on a cellphone captured Brad making a run for it. In the background, you can see what looks like a pile of red and white blankets in the middle of an empty field—that's me—and for just an instant, you see a body blur across the frame. That's Brad, having just realized he was in the line of fire, sprinting across the parking lot to reposition himself behind a cinderblock bathroom next to the Suburban.

There, he had cover, but he was almost as close to the shootout as the people doing the shooting. He could hear the hiss of air going out of punctured tires, the Suburban's glass smashing; he could almost hear Dave taking his slow measured breaths.

Brad saw the muzzle flashes, long tongues of fire leaping off the gunman's rifle barrel, from the building behind home plate.

And then he saw, off to the left, a fearless-looking young woman charging right toward the danger. Over the sounds of gunfire, Brad heard the people near her scream, *"Get down!"* and saw her dive out of view as the gunman turned and fired a burst of rounds that smashed the side of a Lexus she'd tried to take cover behind.

Brad saw another police officer move in behind Dave— this was Officer Kevin Jobe.

Brad saw the gunman emerge from the building behind home plate, with a pistol this time; Brad saw Dave and Officer Jobe returning fire, then closing in, leaving their positions, and moving toward the gunman.

The second Brad heard "Stay down! Don't move!" he was sprinting across the parking lot, toward the field, toward me.

✛ ✛ ✛

Our colleagues yelled from the dugout, "Brad, stay down! Stay down!"

Brad yelled back, "I gotta get to Steve!"

The people in the dugout couldn't see that the threat had been neutralized, that the gunman was now lying on the pavement being cuffed, his guns out of reach.

Brad ignored the yells. At that point, Brad wasn't exactly sure why he felt I was in such peril; it came as much from a kind of sixth sense as it did any medical judgment. It came partially from just the fact that the scene around him was stark: The entire field was empty, a few acres in all directions, and in the middle of it, one unmoving body.

Brad reached me, dropped to his knees, and began talking. Already his mind was moving quickly.

"Hey Steve, so where'd the bullet go in?"

He saw me point to my waist. He moved fabric around and wiped away blood with his hands, still covered by the batting gloves, looking for the wound. He asked me some more questions.

"Steve, can you count to five for me?"

I did.

"Hey Steve, remind me what day it is."

"Wednesday."

"Great. Go ahead and count to five again." To someone else: "Are there scissors?"

Dave had come to me after helping secure the shooter; he knew there was an emergency kit in the Suburban, so he ran to get it and brought it back to Brad, who took the scissors out and started cutting my clothes down the side, looking for the exit wound. He knew to cut the fabric open in such a way that when the time came, he'd have a makeshift hammock to lift me without having to jostle my body much.

As he cut down my pant leg and wiped more blood away,

the entry wound came into view. There was only one wound, in my leg, and it was small. It didn't look bad. It wasn't in my head, after all; it wasn't in my chest. To everyone gathered around, it looked like cause for relief.

Not to Brad. Brad's reaction was the opposite of relief. He was looking at almost the exact same wound he'd seen 10 years before, on that soldier in Iraq who'd become such a burden for him, the one he'd never been able to shake. The same wound in the same part of the body.

In Brad's mind, he was back in Iraq, back at that operating table, standing over a young soldier who appeared to be stable.

Brad did a sweep, running his hands over my body, double-checking, *willing* there to be an exit wound, but he knew it was hopeless. Exit wounds are bigger than entry wounds. If there had been one, he would have seen it right away. It wouldn't have been hard to find. Once he knew the bullet hadn't gone through, he knew it must have gone up.

He worked to keep his voice calm, but he was *seeing* the blood vessels inside me, inside the soldier in Iraq—the two of us fused together, an anatomical drawing of all the critical systems knotted around the trunk of the human body unfolding in his mind's eye. He was thinking about the femoral artery running up my leg, that soldier's leg, the median sacral artery that wraps through the pelvis, the abdominal aorta, the iliac artery that starts around the bottom of the spine and then splits. The iliac especially, because it was a puncture in the iliac, invisible from the outside, that ultimately cost that soldier his life.

Brad imagined the nerve trees, the spine and the spinal cord. He thought about paralysis.

"Hey Steve? Can you move your right leg for me?"

My right leg moved a little.

"Can you move your left leg?"

My left leg didn't seem to move. Brad was now worried about nerve damage but didn't say anything. He was running through the possibilities. He knew what no one else could have known, that I was probably losing way too much of my blood volume, losing even more than whatever I'd bled onto the field. He knew I was in imminent danger of bleeding out. My blood pressure was going to start dropping, which meant, in turn, it was going to start getting harder and harder for my brain to get blood. That meant I was now at imminent risk of brain damage. And then, of death. Brad was the only one who could have seen it. Because he *had* seen it.

He thought of a trick someone had told him about once, when nothing else is available and you're worried about extreme blood loss: He could exsanguinate my arms. He'd hold them up above my head and squeeze them, forcing the blood down from wrist to elbow to shoulder and into my trunk, like a pastry chef squeezing an icing bag. It'd be a way to get the blood I had left to where it was needed most and keep my blood pressure from collapsing.

But if I was beginning to clot—if my blood was beginning to seal up holes on its own—a sudden increase in pressure could blast through the clots like water pressure busting open a damn. He decided against it. He decided that as long as I could talk, he'd assume my brain was getting enough blood. If I lost consciousness, he'd reconsider.

This entire calculation took him a fraction of a second.

Brad was now in a zone—back in a surgical theater at

home in Ohio, at Walter Reed outside D.C., back at a combat hospital in Iraq; the congressmen and police officers gathering around him weren't congressmen and police officers but surgeons and nurses, a surgical support team.

He knew he needed to stop the bleeding. "Somebody give me a belt." Someone gave him a belt. He wrapped it around my leg, above the bullet wound, and pulled tight. One of the officers saw what he was doing and handed him the tactical tourniquets officers carry, a canvas band with a Velcro enclosure and a metal lever to ratchet up the pressure. Brad took it, looped it around my leg and pushed it above the belt, as high up on my leg as he could get it. He applied what was probably the best, tightest, most secure tourniquet ever applied. He wasn't just trying to squeeze off the blood coming out of my leg, he was trying to compress the vessels he was envisioning inside of me, trying to clamp as many of them as far down as he could.

One of the kits someone brought to his side had medical tape, so he started taping the tourniquet down. He found some strange-looking gauze that unrolled both ways, so he put that on too and wrapped it as best as he could. Anything to stop bleeding he could see. Anything to stop bleeding he couldn't see.

"Anybody have a clotting bandage?"

"Maybe in here." Someone handed him another kit, Brad opened it up, and right on top was exactly what he was looking for, a bandage treated with a special chemical that seeps into the blood and helps it clot.

Brad still seemed normal, calm, even though he was moving with great urgency, doing everything he could think of to address injuries no one else could see. The tourniquet was on and seemed to have slowed the external bleeding, a clotting agent was administered, but he knew I'd probably already lost too much blood for him to be at all complacent about my condition. He needed to get fluids in me, to at least begin to replace what I'd lost.

"Steve, you think you can drink?"

Brad had someone get the Gatorade from my bag in the dugout, and he poured it out in front of me. I was on my side, and Brad wouldn't let anyone move me, because even a small move could disrupt the tourniquet or jostle free clots that had begun to form. He liked me on my side, because if I got sick, if I threw up, I wouldn't aspirate. So instead of moving me to let me drink, he poured a stream of Gatorade out in front of me and had me try to catch a little in my mouth.

He knew it wasn't good enough. He knew I had to get fluids in me much faster than that. I needed an IV, but he didn't have one. A couple of drops of Gatorade were enough to give me a little jolt of awareness, but wouldn't do much in the way of replacing the fluids he knew I was losing.

Without an IV, though, there wasn't anything he could do besides the pastry-chef arm trick, which carried the risk of reversing whatever progress I'd made clotting on my own, which meant for the moment, Brad felt stuck, feeling like there wasn't anything else he could do, knowing that whatever it looked like from the outside, he probably hadn't stopped internal bleeding. He knew I needed an IV, and he didn't have one, and without it, I didn't have much longer.

Just then, he heard a voice beside him.

"Hi there."

A man was standing there, dressed in blue, wearing a baseball hat, and dragging a wheeled gurney loaded with a medical kit. It was paramedic and fireman Richard Krimmer. Krimmer knelt down.

"So, what've we got?"

7:17 AM

I hear "Shooter down," and there's a flurry of motion.

I hear—or maybe I feel?—footsteps. They're running to the gunman. I'm not sure how I know that's where they're going, but I know that's where they're going. Conaway has been yelling at me for three minutes, but it feels like Conaway has been whispering gently to me for half an hour.

Anyway, now it's done.

The gunman has been apprehended.

It's all over.

I hear noise, but there are no more gunshots.

I hear that sound which is really the absence of sound, like when a lawnmower shuts off, and you've almost forgotten a lawnmower was on in the first place. The quiet after the engine shuts off, which is somehow more noticeable than the noise of the engine in the first place. *No more gunshots.*

Dave is over me. Brad is over me. All of a sudden, I notice that everybody is over me, all my colleagues pulled in close to me. Brian Kelly is there. He's not wearing a shirt. *Why is your shirt off? Put your shirt back on!*

Brad takes charge. Brad starts asking me questions.

Strange questions, basic questions, questions that have nothing to do with anything.

"How many fingers am I holding up?"

"What day is it?"

"What position are you playing?"

"Can you count to five for me?"

Of course I can count to five, Brad.

He's extremely calm. *Why is Brad so calm? Does he not understand I've been shot?* It seems like Brad and I are just having a conversation—a strange conversation, about extremely, basic things—and his tone is what it might have been had we been discussing the day's vote schedule. Brad is not acting right.

My thoughts are beginning to drift. Strangely, all I can think about is how thirsty I am. *Man,* I'm thirsty.

There's a vague connection between being thirsty and bleeding. It seems logical. "I have a Gatorade bottle in my bag," I say to somebody standing over me; to nobody really. "My bag in the dugout."

Someone runs to the dugout, grabs it, and runs back. They pour the Gatorade slowly out in front of me. I'm holding my mouth open sideways so I can get a little bit of liquid on my tongue. It's mostly puddling on the ground but I'm getting just enough, and there's no better feeling in the world. My mind is searching for things to grab onto to convince itself I'll survive, and that cold liquid becomes one of those things. I feel myself powering up. My energy is coming back. My body was winding down, but now I've convinced myself a thimbleful of Gatorade has saved me. It gives me a little jolt of alertness. I can feel it buying me time. It allows me to remain conscious a little longer. Long enough to feel cutting, air on my skin.

Brad is cutting my clothes.

I don't know what he's doing. I just feel pressure. I can feel pressure even though I also feel numb. I'm feeling something where there's a lack of feeling; this is how logic is starting to break down. Brad is putting pressure where the bullet went in. I see other members around me. Jeff Flake is here, Gary Palmer, Mike Conaway, Dave, a lot of other faces that just kind of blur together and change places. So many people are here! Brad's asking people to get him things. Brad starts talking to me again. We continue our strange little conversation.

7:23 AM

ALEXANDRIA FIRE & EMS

On a quiet side street 500 meters from where I lay bleeding, Safety Officer Wayne Bryant, a long-time veteran of the Alexandria Fire Department, had just come on shift at Station 202 after a four-day vacation. Bryant had the beard scruff to prove it, but he figured it wasn't likely he'd be seeing many of his colleagues that day.

Just after he came on duty, as he was checking the roster for the day, the phone rang. "We're hearing a lot of shots over there at Simpson Field," a woman said.

This was a little unusual. Most people alert authorities by calling 911, not calling fire stations directly. The Alexandria Fire Department usually learns when it's supposed to respond from the Department of Emergency Communications, or DEC, which receives the 911 calls and then sends alerts to first responders over the radio, over an overhead PA system in the fire stations, and through a special network of computers inside the vehicles.

"I don't know what's going on," the caller said, "but there's just a lot of gunshots."

Bryant's first thought was that it was gang-related. His second thought was, *But we don't normally get gang activity early in the morning.* He gathered as much information from the caller as he could get, scribbled it onto a Post-it Note, promised he'd look into it, and hung up.

No sooner had he hung up the phone than a station-wide bell went off, signaling a visitor at the front door.

A woman appeared in the vestibule. "Oh my God," she said, nearly out of breath. "There's people running everywhere, there's shots." She said she couldn't get through to 911.

"How did you get here so fast?"

"I just drove right here. I just drove right past the field and drove right to you."

Another veteran medic at Station 202 named Fiona Apple (yes, like the singer) was also there listening to the woman, and she decided to use the radio to tell other stations what was going on—even though the DEC hadn't officially dispatched them. By then, people had started calling 911, but the DEC had received so many calls in such a short period of time that the lines jammed and callers had started looking for other ways to get help. That actually turned out to be a blessing, because although the Alexandria emergency communication system moved quickly, thanks to concerned citizens, some of the first responders didn't even have to wait for the 911 system, which meant that crucial minutes were shaved off their response time.

A little later, after the woman appeared at the door, after Apple had mobilized, and after she'd gone on the radio to tell other stations what she'd heard, an overhead light in the station lit up red.

Wayne Bryant looked up.

A metallic alarm chirped to life, and an automated female voice came over the loudspeaker. "EMS 202, MEDIC 202!"

"There it is," Bryant said. The DEC was now remotely taking over the station's communications system.

"OPERATE ON TWO DELTA," the voice said, telling them what channel all first responders were to communicate on. "SHOTS FIRED. 426 EAST MONROE." The station house was bathed in the blinking red lights, and simultaneously, all the relevant information was being fed through the MDBs (mobile data browsers), which are laptop-style computers set up inside the vehicles so drivers can jump in the cab, push a button marked "responding," and let the computer guide them to the scene.

But by the time that alert system had spun to life, Station 202 medics had already mobilized, already knew everything the DEC was going to tell them, and were already well on their way.

They'd been given a crucial head start by the most effective early-warning system of all—concerned citizens.

✥ ✥ ✥

Three miles away, and a few minutes earlier, another one of the department's most experienced medics was sitting at a kitchen table in Fire Station 207, listening to the morning conference call with the battalion management team, trying not to look bored.

Richard Krimmer has been doing emergency response for 25 years, with a stint in the middle as a cop, so he has a unique sense of comfort with police. Respectful of the uniform, but—as would be on display later that day—not intimidated by it. He's a medic with a temper; he's been known to yell, to use colorful language when he feels something's getting in his patient's way. He's been known to leave his ambulance in front of a hospital, walk into an emergency room, and give the ER staff an earful when he's worried a kid with a busted arm isn't getting enough attention.

Behind that façade, though, is a guy who grew up wanting to practice medicine, who quietly loved high school science and his classes on gross anatomy, probably would have been a doctor if he hadn't fallen in love with the fire department at 18 years old, and never looked back. He found ways of doctorifying the firefighter and paramedic profession though, taking every extra training he could and even teaching training courses himself. Krimmer taught at a teaching hospital like an accomplished doctor might, providing EMS training at George Washington University.

The morning conference call with the battalion chiefs was droning on when a voice he recognized came over the radio— Fiona Apple over at Station 202, with news of the woman who'd rung their doorbell. "We just had someone walk up to our door and say she heard shots fired over at Simpson Field," Apple said. "We're responding."

Krimmer might otherwise have figured it was some kind of false alarm, but Station 207 where he sat happens to be across from the city's police headquarters, and just as Apple was clicking off the radio, Krimmer could see what looked like a dozen police cars turn on their lights and sirens and peel away from the police station, zooming past his window. It looked like every single officer at morning roll call was being dispatched. Whatever it was that the woman had said over at Station 202, it looked like the police knew about it too.

Something major was happening in Alexandria.

Just like Fiona Apple at 202, at 207, they still didn't have an order to respond. Krimmer felt they didn't need one. He was nearly certain something serious was happening. He made eye contact with his driver Luiz Vasquez.

"Let's just go. Start it up."

They went out to the garage, jumped in, pulled the vehicle out of the station, lit up the sirens, and by the time the MDB in the vehicle chirped to life with the alert that they were supposed to respond to a shooting at Simpson Field, they were just a few minutes from the scene.

✣ ✣ ✣

Krimmer knew there'd likely be a snarl of traffic between the station and the field, and there were a dozen or so traffic lights along the way. Sirens provide encouragement for cars to get out of the way, but can't force them. Sirens help you go through a red light, but you still have to slow down. And if cars are lined up at an intersection, there's not always space to go around them. Sirens *ask* cars to move over; they can't make traffic disappear into thin air. If there's no place for cars to go, or if a driver has his radio turned up too loud or is just late to work and doesn't feel like budging, ambulances slow down. Ambulances can't fly. And Alexandria is one of the most popular places to live for people who work in Washington. In the morning, everyone crowds onto the beltway to begin the crawl toward the city.

At 7:14 AM, a police officer came over the radio, yelling, "We've got one in custody!"

This was Officer Jobe, radioing from the field.

"One shooter. We need medics!"

It was right around that time that Krimmer noticed something strange: the roads were totally clear. It should have been bumper to bumper, but for some reason, the route between the station and the field was empty. It seemed abandoned. Somehow, every single traffic light turned green just as they were approaching. They hit only green the whole way. Krimmer looked over at his driver each time it happened. It was almost funny. They made it in half the time Krimmer expected it to take. At right around 7:23 AM, they were already pulling into a lot by the field.

Vasquez parked the ambulance in the lot between the backstop and the YMCA, right next to where the gunman had parked his van.

Krimmer took a beat to make sure he was prepared, to get his equipment ready, check that his A-bag was full of bandages, and set up the oxygen and the Lifepak with the cardiac monitor. The closest patient was the gunman, but he was already being tended to; he'd be pronounced dead soon after. Krimmer walked up to the crowd standing over him.

"Who else needs help?"

An officer pointed toward the Suburban.

Krimmer went over to the vehicle and saw firemen standing over a woman holding her leg. That was Crystal.

Crystal was badly wounded. Her ankle had been shattered; she needed help. But she was sitting up and talking. Krimmer was underwhelmed.

"So is there—I'm sorry, but is there somebody worse off than this?"

Krimmer hoped his voice sounded polite. Someone shrugged and pointed toward the field.

That's when Krimmer came to me.

✛ ✛ ✛

Krimmer saw a man in a baseball uniform who seemed to have taken charge and who introduced himself as a doctor. This was Brad Wenstrup. He did not tell Krimmer he was a congressman.

Brad explained he'd put a tourniquet on, but he seemed adamant about one thing, something that didn't immediately make sense. He said, "I'm having trouble stopping the bleeding."

Krimmer was looking down at the wound. The wound didn't seem to be bleeding.

Krimmer looked at my face. He thought I looked pale; he thought I looked like I was in pain. But still: the wound wasn't bleeding. It was apparent that the tourniquet was working. He stored this disconnect to deal with later.

Brad said, "How quickly can you start an IV?"

"I don't have one; I can't do that out here."

That wasn't entirely true. Krimmer *could* have started an IV out on the field, but the back of his medic unit is (usually) a more comfortable place for him to work, and there was a lot of rough ground between where I lay, on the field, and the ambulance. If he took the time to start an IV on the field only to have it be ripped out as they rolled me back to the ambulance, it'd end up costing time, not saving it.

Krimmer said, "Let's lift him up and get him off the ball field."

Using the makeshift hammock Brad had cut out of my uniform, they lifted me onto the stretcher and began wheeling me back to the medic unit, taking a different route out, because even in the very short period of time during which Krimmer was with me on the field, the parking lot had been cordoned off with caution tape and armed personnel. It turned out Krimmer and Vasquez had parked their ambulance in what was only now very obviously the middle of a crime scene.

As they were rushing me back to the ambulance, someone asked Krimmer, "Do you need a helicopter?"

"Give me a minute to see what I have, but yes, I think we will."

Then Krimmer, along with his driver and a supervisor who'd shown up to help, loaded me into the vehicle, and Krimmer got to work.

He asked me what my name was.

He heard me say, "Steve."

"Okay Steve, we're gonna take good care of you."

He checked the tourniquet to make sure it hadn't slipped or come loose while they'd run me across the field. It was still tight and secure. Still no bleeding.

He reached for an IV line, and suddenly, Krimmer realized we weren't alone.

He'd been so focused on getting me into the ambulance and getting to work that he hadn't realized his ambulance had been essentially occupied by a bunch of armed men he didn't recognize. They looked like Secret Service, or Capitol Police, he didn't know; all he knew was that none of them were firemen or medics. I was a member of congress. He didn't know it was an entire field full of members of Congress that had come under attack. The fact that there were armed men all over his ambulance made no sense and immediately annoyed him. They were getting in his way. He wasn't worried about who his patient was, he was worried about how the patient was doing, and he knew the interior of his medic unit like an extension of himself. He knew it by feel; he knew, almost without having to look, where everything was.

For the first of several times throughout the day, the people trying to save my life and the people trying to protect me had to find ways of working together.

Krimmer barked for one of the men to move back into a corner.

He yelled for another to get over on the wheel well. He told them all to get as far away from him, and from me, as they could possibly get, to become part of the walls.

Then he got back to work. Brad's words still hung out there. He had tried to impress upon Krimmer how important it was that I get fluids into me as soon as possible—that's why Brad made it clear he was a doctor and didn't even bother saying he was a congressman. He wanted the paramedic to take what he said seriously.

Krimmer had paid attention, even though he often doesn't pay much mind to what bystanders say, because he often comes across domineering bystanders feigning some kind of medical prowess. In this case, there was a dissonance—a doctor expressing so much concern about bleeding when there was *no apparent bleeding*—that loosened from the recesses of Krimmer's mind a fact that he knew and had, actually, always been intrigued by. A curiosity of the human body he'd heard about in an anatomy class or textbook once and that had stuck with him—that you can bleed half of your blood volume into your pelvis. Which means that you can bleed to death without anyone seeing a drop of blood.

The handoff between Brad Wenstrup and Richard Krimmer could have gone any number of ways. Brad could have been unclear; Krimmer could have just ignored him as he took over; Krimmer could have failed to hear or compute, over the commotion, the hint Brad was trying to get him to see. But Krimmer was uniquely suited to register the counterintuitive notion that I was bleeding *into* my body. I was handed over from a doctor who'd seen an almost identical wound to a paramedic with an almost obsessive level of interest in human anatomy, so the nonobvious fact that my life was in imminent danger survived the transfer.

Krimmer didn't need any more of a hint than the one Brad gave. Even though Krimmer couldn't see any bleeding, he began treating me for blood loss.

He started an IV, started giving me fluids to try and keep my blood pressure from bottoming out, and, critically, gave me TXA, tranexamic acid, a chemical that helps prevent clots from breaking down.

I started to make noise again, mumbling, stirring. He gave me pain medication and checked my entire body to make sure there weren't any other injuries he hadn't seen.

He checked the tourniquet again, since he'd moved me around. Somebody opened the rear door of the medic unit and asked, again, "So, do you want a helicopter?"

"Yes."

Krimmer hurried to get me ready for the transfer. He knew time was of the essence. He knew I had to get to a hospital quickly, and he didn't want to waste crucial seconds by making the helicopter wait. He rushed to pack up all the equipment that was going to travel with me and to secure it so it wouldn't jostle or fall when they moved me.

He shifted me onto a hard board to make moving my body to another gurney easier.

He checked and then rechecked that the fluid was still flowing and that the IVs were secure, so they wouldn't get ripped out in the chaos of the transition. And as soon as he heard the thumping outside that indicated the helicopter was landing, he checked one last time that the tourniquet was still secure.

He could hear by the change in the timbre of the rotors that the helicopter had settled down somewhere behind him, and he hurried to finish getting me ready for transport.

Then he heard the helicopter spin up and take off without me.

✥ ✥ ✥

While Krimmer had been racing toward the field from Station 207, astounded by the series of green lights and clear roads, Wayne Bryant was on his way from Station 202, just four blocks away.

As Bryant hurried out to his vehicle, he remembered, *I've played softball on this field!* He knew a back way. Since most of the responders were sure to follow the address automatically sent to the computers in all the vehicles, all converging at that one point, he figured he'd go a different way and avoid the bottleneck. So Bryant ignored the GPS and followed a back way toward a small parking lot, off the left field fence. When he got there, he saw more and more people beginning to show up and could hear sirens of still more incoming emergency response vehicles. It was already turning into a crowded scene. He reached up to his beard scruff. *Damn.*

Sure enough, the fire chief arrived.

The assistant chief arrived.

All his superiors showed up. Just about every single one of his colleagues was there to see him looking like he was still on leave.

Oh well. Time to get to work. Bryant surveyed the scene. His first task, as safety officer, was to make sure all the medics were safe. At a violent scene, that means making sure they stay back in a staging area and don't commit themselves to patients before there's an "all clear" call. It means making sure they stay back until the fire's been put out, the gunman's been put down, the coast rendered clear.

Once the medics start treating patients, Bryant becomes an extra set of eyes and ears, making sure they're okay. If, and only if, he's confident the medics are safe, then he becomes a kind of free agent. He doesn't have to stick to a crew like everyone else; he tries to identify who needs the most help, and he goes to help them.

The fire battalion chief had called for an EMS task force, which meant at least five ambulances were inbound, and with other jurisdictions responding too and ambulances coming in even from the airport, Bryant could see that every patient was being taken care of.

He went over to the incident commander to ask what else he could do to help.

"We've got critical patients. We've got helicopters inbound, but the police don't want anyone landing on the baseball field. It's a crime scene. They want to preserve the crime scene."

"You want me to set up an LZ"—a landing zone— "somewhere else?"

The commander looked around, then gestured toward a patch of green nestled up against the highway bridge. "How about up there on the soccer field?"

"Copy that."

Bryant ran up to the soccer field. He brought bolt cutters for locked gates, hard helmets, and eye protection for anyone who was going to be nearby, and cones to mark the area for the incoming pilot. He put on his neon vest and went out into the middle of the street, trying to use his body to block off traffic coming down from the highway ramp.

An Alexandria police officer walked up to him.

"Hey! You setting up the LZ?"

"Yessir, trying to block off this ramp. I gotta keep these cars away."

"Okay," the officer said. He nodded toward another officer. "We'll help."

One of them moved the cruiser up to the ramp and blocked it off, and they sealed off a wide swath of the field to give the chopper a big, flat area to land on without any hazards and without disturbing the crime scene.

On cue, Bryant heard the thumping of a helicopter lowering itself toward the ground.

Except the sound was coming from behind him.

He and the fire chief both turned around and together saw the helicopter descending—right onto the baseball field.

"What the—?"

The chief radioed the Medevac helicopter. "You're landing on the wrong field!! What're you doing?! Pull up!"

There was a pause before the pilot's voice came back over the radio. "Uh, sir, we're not landing."

"We *just* said don't land on the baseball field! It's a crime scene! We have bullets and shell casings everywhere!"

"That's not us. We're still inbound."

Bryant and his chief looked at each other. *Then who the hell is landing on the crime scene?*

Since the first responders didn't know (nor would they have particularly cared) that among the victims were members of Congress, they hadn't anticipated the feds. The feds, however, had known something was going down on the baseball field from the moment Crystal had gotten on the radio in the Suburban and called for help. The Capitol Police and the Park Police can self-dispatch. They don't need to wait for the Department of Emergency Communications to decide who should respond, so as soon as Crystal had said congressmen were under fire, the Capitol Police coordinated with the Park Police to get a chopper in the air.

At the field, Bryant and the Alexandria Fire Department had even more help incoming than they knew.

But since *they* didn't know congressmen had been under fire, they didn't know, and hadn't anticipated, that the feds had sent a chopper. So, of course, it never occurred to them to tell an incoming chopper they didn't know was coming where to land.

The fact that the Park Police beat the normal helicopters there was a small blessing, even though they didn't see the perfect, non–crime scene landing zone Bryant had so pains-takingly set up. Having a Park Police helicopter was key, because Washington, D.C., has the most secure airspace in the country. The agency that keeps it secure is the Park Police, so their own helicopters can get around the city the fastest.

But because the Park Police helicopter wasn't there on request from the Alexandria Fire Department, they weren't told who the most critical patients were, so when the heli-copter landed, the flight medic just looked around to see who needed help the most.

I was out of sight, off in an ambulance with Krimmer (who was getting me ready for a helicopter).

Crystal was right there, just 20 feet off the baseball field. They saw Crystal, loaded her onto the bird, spun up, and took off.

✤ ✤ ✤

From inside the medic unit, Krimmer heard the sound of a helicopter—*his* helicopter—taking off.

Krimmer lost his temper.

He didn't know it'd been a Park Police helicopter, rather than a MedStar helicopter. What he knew was that he had the most critical patient on the scene.

After screaming at no one in particular, he said to the offi-cers still inside the vehicle, "Get me to a hospital. Just give me a driver right now." Krimmer wanted Vasquez in back with him, helping to treat me. "Hey! Get me another driver. Put a driver in the front seat and get me to a hospital."

"Which hospital you want to go to?"

"We'll go to GW. I don't care. Let's just get on the road."

Someone got up in the cab, and the ambulance took off.

And then, almost immediately, it stopped.

Krimmer heard the driver roll down the window, and he could overhear the conversation. "Who've you got in back?"

It took a minute to get waved on, and then they were on their way.

Krimmer felt the ambulance come to a halt *again*.

He overheard another version of the same conversation and was beginning to lose his temper again. The crime scene had been closed off around the ambulance, so now they were effectively escaping a crime scene.

Finally, the officer allowed the ambulance to pass.

A *third* time they were stopped. Krimmer lost it. He screamed at the driver, "Hey buddy! If one more person steps in front of you, you run 'em over and we'll treat him later!"

The ambulance started again, and he felt the vehicle stop a *fourth* time. This time, the *back* doors swung open. Krimmer turned to give the officer standing there a piece of his mind at the top of his lungs, "Tell your guys to get the—"

"The helicopter's coming back! You want to fly him out?"

"Yes, I want to fly him out!"

"Why are we screaming?!" Only then could Krimmer hear the rotors thumping again.

"Where's the flight medic?"

"He'll meet you at the helicopter!"

✜ ✜ ✜

By that point the ambulance hadn't made it far. They'd barely made it out of the parking lot, but the few hundred feet of progress they *had* made put them as close to where the helicopter landed as they could possibly have been, without driving up onto the field.

This time, Safety Officer Bryant was happy to see the helicopter coming down in the landing zone he'd made.

Krimmer covered me up and wheeled me to the side door of the chopper. They spun the gurney around to load me headfirst, lifted the hard board off the gurney, and transferred me inside.

Then, just as a few minutes before Brad had made sure Krimmer didn't miss the gravity of my condition, Krimmer made sure the flight medic didn't, either. Krimmer yelled at the top of his lungs, to make sure the medic could hear over the sound of rotors, through his flight helmet and ear protection, to make sure the medic knew how serious my condition was.

As the helicopter lifted off, Krimmer went back to the ambulance.

He still didn't know who any of us were, other than that my name was Steve and that, for some reason, the entire federal government seemed to have shown up. All he knew was that he needed to be ready to respond to other emergencies.

He closed the ambulance doors and started fiddling with a stubborn lock, cursing it, throwing a small fit, the way you do when you're frustrated by a stuck zipper or backpack strap caught in a chair castor and no one's around to see you lose it—or at least, you don't *think* anyone's around to see you.

As the thump of the helicopter rotor blades got quieter, the helicopter racing toward the MedStar Washington Hospital Center, Krimmer heard his phone ringing. His wife was calling.

"Are you in the middle of this?"

"How'd you know that?"

"Well, Mom and Dad just saw you on TV."

On TV—How...?

He turned, slowly, phone still to his ear, and for the first time, he saw that up above him, lining the highway bridge, was a mass of bodies, cameramen and correspondents with microphones, photographers with huge telephoto lenses, standing on the bridge, all facing down toward him.

Oh, boy.

7:26 AM

I hear Brad's voice saying, "Do you have an IV?"

I'm still so thirsty that when I hear "IV" I think, *Ooh, yeah, IV sounds good.*

I realize Brad is talking to a paramedic. That means a paramedic has arrived. That has to be good.

I hear the paramedic say, "No."

That has to be bad.

I start to get frustrated.

It feels like I've been lying on this field for an hour.

Then I say, or I think, "I don't want to bleed out on this field."

I hear the paramedics come. But then I remember the paramedics have already come. Didn't they already come?

Didn't Brad just ask them for an IV?

How long have they been here?

Why am I still on the field?

Are they going to let me bleed out on the field?

Out of the corner of my eye, I see Senator Jeff Flake. Jeff is a steady guy, a good guy, and I see him at the same moment I realize things are very serious and I'm not getting the help I need.

Okay, wait.

I'm thinking of my wife. I need to call Jen. The only thing I'm thinking very clearly about is that I need Jen to know I'm okay.

Or that I'm not okay, but I'm not dying.

Or that I may be dying, but I'm not dead. My phone is on

my seat in the Suburban. I give Jeff the code to unlock it. Jeff leaves.

More time passes, 10 minutes, 20 minutes, maybe an hour. I'm still on the field. *What's taking so long?*

I hear a helicopter. I'm being moved. They must be bringing me to the helicopter.

I feel myself being loaded into a helicopter.

But it must be a slow helicopter, because it doesn't feel like it's moving very fast. It feels like it's barely moving at all. It feels like it keeps stopping. I could swear I'm in a helicopter that's standing perfectly still.

Things are becoming blurry.

Motion again, this thing is moving—for a moment. Then the motion stops. The doors are swinging open. I must be at the hospital.

The hospital looks—like a baseball field.

I'm back on the baseball field.

What the hell is going on here?

I'm not in the helicopter at all. Even in my confused state, as nearly all of my faculties leave me, I register the fact that it is very, very bad, that after all that, I'm right back where I started. Have I totally lost it? Is this Groundhog Day? Am I doomed to relive a nightmare over and over?

"What's going on?" I ask. "Why am I not at a hospital yet?"

I'm impatient, I'm as frustrated as I am scared, and also, I'm very, very tired. "Take me somewhere. Take me anywhere. I don't care where you take me. Just take me to a hospital. I don't want to bleed out on this field."

I say this to someone, or to a bunch of people, or maybe I just think it. "Just take me to a hospital. I don't care which one, okay? Do you hear me? Does anyone hear?"

It's these peaks of frustration, of surliness, that keep me alert. A little stab of frustration, every once in a while, that gets me riled. It's saving me, because it's now nearly impossible to hold on to any one thought. I think something, and then it passes, slides through my grasp and disappears, like a note with the thing I want to remember fluttering out of my hand. In my mind, I go chasing after it, but I can never quite catch it. Frustration is turning into resignation though; I can feel it happening. I'm beginning to feel like it's slipping away. I feel so astoundingly weak. And I feel, this is probably it.

I ask the person standing over me for his phone. Or her phone. I'm not really distinguishing between driver and paramedic, fireman and pilot, man and woman. I'm thinking, *I need to speak to my wife.* I'm exhausted. Everything is shutting down. I know this is all bad; it's all really, really bad. Jen needs to hear my voice. Jen needs to hear my voice, and she needs to hear it right now, because it might be the last time she ever will. *I need a phone.* Did I just ask for a phone? There's a phone in my hand. Somehow, I'm able to recite her number. I can hear it ringing.

Jen, please, pick up. I need to talk to you. Please, please Jen, just pick up.

The phone rings once, twice, but there's no answer. She doesn't pick up. *Jen, please.*

It goes to voicemail. I leave the kind of message you leave for someone you love when you know you'll never see them again. When you want to say exactly what they need to know, so you just open up your heart. I leave her a message she won't hear, won't even know is there, for almost a week, and that she will never, ever share with anyone. And that's the last thing I remember, before I fade off into oblivion.

Everything goes dark.

Spring, 2008

THE FRESHMAN

On that very field, years before, is where I first began to feel like maybe, just maybe, I belonged in this town.

I'd just arrived in Washington, D.C., and I hardly knew anyone. It was like the first day of junior high. Even more awkward than that, really. I was like the kid who transfers into the new junior high halfway through the school year and doesn't even get to be lost and awkward with the other lost and awkward kids.

It was 2008, and I'd come into Congress from a special election. Bobby Jindal had just stepped down in the middle of a congressional term to become governor, so we had an election at a time when no one else in the country was having an election. Rather than joining Congress with a whole class of freshmen going through orientation and learning the ropes together, I came in alone. I didn't even have a place to live. I had to call a childhood friend, a guy I'd roomed with in college. "Jack! So, uh, I just got elected to Congress! But I need a place to stay...."

Jack had a spare room, it turned out, because he and his wife were getting ready to have a baby.

So I had one friend, who wasn't even in Congress, and a place to stay in a crib room, about to be evicted by a newborn.

Jim McCrery, then the dean of the Louisiana delegation and a very respected member of Congress, had quickly become a mentor of mine; I turned to him for advice on just about everything those first few months. During a vote series on the House floor just a few weeks in, I sought him out to help me with my housing issue.

"Hey Jim, so, uh, where do you live?"

He looked at me.

"I'm looking around for places. If you want to buy a place, it's almost a million dollars! I mean, the *real estate* in this city...."

"John Shimkus has an opening at his townhouse."

"Oh, great," I said. Only, there was one problem. "Um, so, who's John Shimkus?"

Jim raised his eyebrows and pointed across the floor. "There's John."

Aha. John was a member of Congress. Boy, did I have a lot to learn.

After casting my vote, I walked across the floor to the guy Jim had pointed to.

"Hey there, are you John? I'm Steve Scalise. Jim McCrery told me you have an opening at your townhouse?"

"I sure do! You want to come take a look?"

We arranged for me to stop by that night after dinner. It was a four-bedroom townhouse out by the Potomac, just five minutes from the Capitol, and one of the members had just moved out right as I was coming in off my special election, so the timing just happened to work out. I called Jen that night. "The place is great, close to the Capitol, right on the river, and the price is right."

I told John I'd take the room, and moved in the very next day. The move didn't take long. I didn't have many belongings up in Washington with me.

Early in the morning, after my first night there, I heard

rumbling outside my bedroom door. I got up to see what was going on. For a moment, it looked like the guys were all wearing tights.

"Steve!" John said, "You coming to practice?"

"Practice for what?

"For the baseball game."

"For what baseball game?"

"For the—why don't you just get your glove?"

"I don't have a glove."

I hadn't heard of the Congressional Baseball Game. I certainly hadn't known I was joining a house in which all my new roommates played, and I hadn't known that my new landlord was actually kind of a big deal (as big a deal as middle-aged men playing baseball can get). John was the Republicans' best pitcher, the MVP a bunch of years running. He explained how every summer, after a few weeks of practice, we got to play a game in a Major League baseball stadium. I didn't need much more convincing than that. I'd gone to a college that has one of the best NCAA baseball teams in the country, and a lot of *those* guys never got to play in a Major League park. It had a *Revenge of the Nerds* appeal.

And speaking of nerds, what really sold me, at least as much as the chance to take the field at Nationals Park, was the chance to actually, finally, start making some friends and getting to know colleagues.

✢ ✢ ✢

I didn't have a glove, so I borrowed one.

I didn't have a position, so I borrowed one of those too.

I was just getting to know one of my new roommates, Kevin Brady, and though I wouldn't even have known his name had we not just become housemates, I quickly established a kinship with him. He's from Houston, and I was in the Louisiana State House when Hurricane Katrina struck New Orleans. Houston took in a lot of our people, so I'd always been grateful to the whole city. I got to know Brady a little quicker than I got to know anyone else, and when Brady saw me wandering the field like a fish out of water, he took pity. "Scalise! Here, come on, I'll show you how to play infield."

He was the starting second baseman, so he put me at shortstop, where I'd be closest to him and he could coach me along.

Over the next few weeks, as we got closer to the big game, he began to teach me the fundamentals. I'd never played real organized baseball before, only the sandlot-style free-for-all, and even then, it had mostly been softball. This was fast-pitch baseball, so it was new to me. With Kevin's help, I began to learn the correct way to position yourself when a ground ball was coming at you and how to transfer the ball from your glove to your throwing hand fast enough to turn a double play or throw out a fast base runner (there isn't exactly a wealth of fast base runners in the Congressional Baseball Game, so it's all relative). Most of all, I was learning that baseball was a really good way to build relationships. And while I knew it felt good to finally be meeting congressmen, I didn't realize until later how well baseball actually served my career. I was just beginning to think about which committee assignments interested me and how best to get them. I began to see more clearly that if I ever led anything—if I ever chaired a committee, for example—I didn't have that master manipulator, chess grandmaster skills some politicians do. I didn't really have the ability to intimidate. I'm probably too easily amused; I laugh too much to scare anyone. I don't have a booming voice that strikes fear into the hearts of dissenting congressmen.

I was beginning to understand that the way I might be able to be effective as a leader was by doing what, as a native Louisianan, came naturally to me: building relationships over good, Southern cooking.

The strategy had been there all along, it just took a while for me to realize it: You can learn just about all you need to know about a person by sharing a few dozen charbroiled oysters from Drago's. When it comes time to bring people together to vote or to try and get them to agree on some proposal or another, the old way of doing that was threatening to take away their committee postings, kill projects in their districts, or endorse their primary opponents.

But another way was just trying to listen to people, so you could write laws that had a better chance of appealing to them in the first place. Because you actually *know* them. And it's easier to know people if you've broken bread with them, if you've shared some good food and wine.

Or if you've played baseball with them.

There's a limit to how well you can get to know someone during business hours when you're all wearing suits and ties, but when you spend time around a bunch of guys pretending they're young again (never having looked more their advanced ages)—you bond. Once I started going to the baseball practices, it was like the gates to an exclusive club opened up. Much more so, believe it or not, than being elected to Congress in the first place.

Waking up early to play a kid's game was starting to feel really good; it felt therapeutic, and it was helping me make new friends. When someone threw a ball to me, he didn't have time to think, *I'm throwing the ball to the new guy who doesn't know what he's doing and looks awkward when I see him in the halls of Congress wandering around like a lost puppy.* He wasn't throwing to a freshman member; he was throwing to a teammate.

Everyone seemed keen to teach me something new. When I decided the throw from shortstop to first was too long for me, I moved to second base but still felt my arm strength left something to be desired. So Shimkus took me aside and coached my mechanics so I could get some force behind the throw. Everyone was eager to help.

I got to know people I otherwise would never have gotten to know so well. People like Rand Paul, a Libertarian in the Senate I'd have had little opportunity to interact with otherwise. People like Jeff Flake, a congressman and then senator from Arizona, a state that doesn't have a great deal in common with mine. And I think it was a way I began to earn respect from my colleagues. I don't know that anyone ever really respected my athletic background—there wasn't much there to respect in the first place. But I like to think my hustle spoke for itself.

✛ ✛ ✛

Every season after that first year, I was out there on the first day of practice—out there hustling like the overeager kid who answers all the questions in chemistry class and then asks for extra homework. First in, last out.

When the games came, I didn't get to play much, but it was still a thrill to be out in the dugout at Nationals Park, and every once in a while, I came in to play when the game was already out of hand, our team already winning or losing by so much any mistakes I made wouldn't much matter. It was still a thrill. It never gets old, walking out onto the field and hearing the roar of a crowd in a 41,000-seat stadium—even if only a few thousand of those seats were actually occupied. The little I got to play was unlike anything I'd done before. I learned the secret to what makes Major League fielders look so good. I'm convinced it's not just superior hand–eye coordination; it's that those fields are as smooth as glass! The ball never takes a bad hop. Everything is perfectly predictable. Ground balls come right to you.

I ended up developing a niche role: I became a pinch-running specialist. If one of our slower batters got on base, I'd sub in for him, because I was willing to run my tail off. Pinch-running became my forte. Pete Sessions, a fellow congressman, started saying, "Scalise, if you get on base, you score!"

Then one day after a practice three years ago, right before the game, the coach came out to the dugout to read off the starting lineup. It was the very same week I suddenly found myself elected to the position of majority whip. Coach held up a position sheet to read out the starters. He went through each position, but when he got to second base, he didn't say what he always said, which was "Kevin Brady at second base."

Instead, he said, "Steve Scalise at second base."

I nearly screamed. For a moment, it felt like I'd made the big leagues. I was starting.

✤ ✤ ✤

The most important thing about playing in the baseball game is getting a rare chance to embarrass Cedric Richmond.

I represent Louisiana's first congressional district; Cedric represents the second. I'm the conservative Republican; he's the liberal Democrat. I'm the majority whip, and he's the chairman of the Congressional Black Caucus. We'd been close friends ever since we were both neophytes in Louisiana state politics, a world with enough bare-fisted toughness to scare a prize-fighter away, and where a true friend is invaluable, regardless of what party he or she belongs to.

On the baseball field, we were rivals, partially because Cedric was so darned good. He played baseball in college, and he was by far the best player in the Congressional Baseball Game, which, of course, I would never admit to his face.

In the 2011 game, Cedric was pitching a no-hitter through six innings; we just could not catch up to his fastball. Every time he came off the mound after mowing down our batters, fans chanted, "MVP! MVP!"

By the next year, Cedric's dominance in the Congressional Baseball Game had become a *thing*. The Democrats' coach called him "The Franchise." People in the stands held up billboards with his name on it; one young woman held up one that said:

"REP. RICHMOND. CALL ME MAYBE"

Even our own coach publicly admitted to Cedric's greatness, giving a quote for the official game program (on which the cover was a photo of, you guessed it, Cedric Richmond) that read: "In the almost 30 years I've been involved with the game, he is the best Congressman to play in the game."

I wasn't going to be intimidated by all the hype. I came up that game in the bottom of the second inning. One Republican had walked to get on base, and everyone was expecting Cedric to get me out on the way to another dominant complete game.

A high fast ball came in; I swung and crushed a line drive right over the second baseman's head, far enough into right-center field that the base runner scored. I was ecstatic. It was a Disney movie, David slaying Goliath moment, ending Cedric's bid for a no-hitter even before it really began and driving in a run at the same time. I whooped and clapped as I ran, savoring the moment, getting to first base and pumping my fists.

Cedric, surprisingly, responded to my antics by congratulating me. He came over toward the base and said, "Damn, did you have to hit it so hard?"

Democrats in the stands weren't as gracious. They responded to my minor triumph with a "We Got Health Care" chant.

A few years later, with Cedric pitching yet *another* complete game, I had one more chance for greatness.

I was watching him closely, and by that point, I felt I knew his game well enough to know when his form was breaking down with fatigue. I got on base late in the game and managed to steal second, then third.

From third base, I could tell Cedric was beginning to wear down. The summer heat and the weight of carrying his team were finally getting to him in those later innings; his mechanics began to slip.

I taunted him with an almost boastfully big lead, trying to get in his head, *daring* him to look my way, to try and pick me off. And, crucially, distracting him from the batter he should have been paying more attention to.

When he threw the pitch, it went well off the mark, far enough from the strike zone that it got past the catcher and hopped toward the backstop.

I took off running. I ran as hard as I've ever run in my life, pumping my arms and legs as hard as I could, hardly breathing, crossing home before the catcher could get the ball back to home plate to tag me out. The umpire yelled, "Safe!"

I'd stolen home plate on Cedric!

The crowd went wild, and even if the statisticians would, technically, categorize the play as an error and not a stolen base, what mattered to me, the crowd, and Cedric was that I'd bested him. It was the highlight of my baseball career, stealing home on the MVP, the Democrats' ringer, "best player in the game" no one would ever shut up over, repping Louisana's first to Louisiana's second, shoving it in the face of the dominant prodigal son, who always gets all the glory.

What made that second Goliath-slaying moment even better was that a photographer captured the moment, me sprinting down the baseline, forehead scrunched with all-out effort, Cedric running to cover home plate, with a grin that said, "Damn, I'm never gonna live this one down." I, naturally, had the picture blown up to an obnoxiously large size and then hung it in the Lincoln Room, a part of the whip's office once occupied by Abraham Lincoln himself.

I wanted everyone to see me getting the best of Cedric.

✣ ✣ ✣

Even as a conservative congressman, the biggest clash I've had with a Democrat was probably on the base path. Lacy Clay, a congressman from St. Louis, tried to steal second, and I moved over to take the throw from the catcher. I caught the ball and turned to lay a tag down on the sliding base runner—only the base runner wasn't sliding. Clay came barreling at me, upright, showing no indication that he was looking to avoid contact at all. He barreled right into me, two not-so-youthful bodies crashing together and barely staying intact, but somehow, after the dust settled, one man was on the ground and one was left standing.

As I pulled the ball out of my glove, I looked down at Lacy recovering, and I held the ball up in the air. The umpire rumbled over, looked at me, checked that I had the ball, and threw up his fist. *"YOU'RE OUT!"*

A *Roll Call* photographer caught that one too. Baseball wasn't just giving me friends; it was giving me moments I'd never forget!

Of course, the noteworthy moments weren't always triumphant ones. *Roll Call* also immortalized my more embarrassing moments, the times Cedric got the better of me.

Cedric came out with a wooden bat one game, and as he walked up to the plate, I thought, *Wait a minute, I recognize that bat.* On the barrel, there was a familiar inscription:

SCALISE WHIP TEAM 2014
BRING THE WOOD

What in the——?

I yelled from the dugout.

"That's my bat!"

Cedric had somehow managed to pilfer one of the souvenirs I'd had Marucci make for my whip team and that I'd handed out the night before the leadership vote. How'd he get that?! How'd a Democrat get one of the *Republican* whip team bats?

Cedric could hear me screaming from the dugout, and he just smiled his thousand-megawatt smile. I yelled, "That bat is *not* to be used in the game!"

Fortunately, we walked him, and he pretty much knew we were going to, so he never planned to swing the bat anyway. As much as he would've loved to run up the trash talking score by smashing a home run with my own whip team bat, I knew that deep down, he would never have jeopardized fine Louisiana craftsmanship to do so.

"To beat Republicans," he said, "we don't need to use it."

7:30 AM

JENNIFER SCALISE

At the field, from the back of an ambulance, I was desperately trying to reach my wife.

I'd borrowed someone's phone, a policeman's, a paramedic's; I wasn't sure. I only knew one thing. I had to talk to Jen. I dialed her as the corners closed in, just as I started going into shock.

Jen woke to the phone buzzing on the bedside table. The moment she opened her eyes she had the dejected, annoyed feeling you get when you're overtired. The feeling like you've only just fallen asleep, seconds ago, and some inconsiderate thing's already come along to rouse you.

Can't you just let me have 30 more minutes?

It was 6:30 in New Orleans. Her alarm was set to go off in half an hour, and she'd been up late the night before, getting the house and the kids ready to travel in a couple of days. She groped around on the night table for the phone and pulled it in front of her face. The caller ID said, "Alexandria, Virginia."

She didn't know anyone from Alexandria, Virginia.

She felt a little sliver of rage.

A wrong number at 6:30 in the morning?!

She slammed the phone down on the nightstand without answering and tried to go back to sleep.

Up in Virginia, my heart sank, as I heard my call go to voicemail. Around me, other players heard me leave the message, or heard that I'd asked for a phone to speak with my wife—and thought I actually had. Teammates at the practice began updating their staff back at the Capitol, staff back at the Capitol began updating other members, and soon even people in my own office had heard and begun sharing the news that I was doing just fine. They didn't know I was going into shock, and that I was minutes from dying. I'd just been hit in the leg, it was minor, I was alert, they all thought. I was speaking to my wife.

✤ ✤ ✤

Down in New Orleans, Jen's phone buzzed with a voicemail.

Are you kidding?

Two minutes later, it buzzed again.

Who keeps calling? Leave me alone!

She grabbed the phone, ready to throw it against a wall, and saw my caller ID photo on the screen.

Suddenly the missed call made sense. Wasn't my baseball practice in Alexandria?

Now she was wide awake.

She ripped the phone off the charging cord, ran out of the room, and practically flew down the stairs, feet barely touching them. She found herself huddled in the laundry room, the farthest place in the house from where our kids were sleeping. Even then—seconds after waking up and nearing panic because with me calling that early, she knew something must be wrong—she was thinking several steps ahead about how to protect our kids. She closed the door and answered the phone.

"Steve? Are you okay?"

"Jennifer, this is Jeff Flake."

While I was in the ambulance, Jeff was outside, calling Jen from my phone. Jen's mind was still scrolling through worst-case scenarios and wasn't immediately placing faces with the names of all 535 members of Congress. *Jeff Flake?*

"I'm at baseball practice with Steve."

Who is this? Jeff Flake must be some new intern or something.

"Okay...."

Jen could hear that Jeff was breathing heavily, and she heard commotion behind him. She heard voices in the background, voices getting louder, other voices getting quieter, like they belonged to people who were moving with urgency. She pictured people running. She knew something was wrong. She felt she knew what it was: I'd had a heart attack.

"Hello, Jennifer? I'm at pract—"

"Where's Steve?"

Jeff was silent for a moment. "Do you have the news on?"

"No, I don't have the news on. Where's Steve? I don't have the news on. Tell me what's going on."

"Well, there was a shooter at practice this morning."

Jen fell to her knees.

"Let me talk to Steve."

"Well, uh—they're working with him right now. He's been hit."

✛ ✛ ✛

At that moment, something strange happened. Jen describes it as a gift from God, albeit one that came in a strange form.

Just as Jeff was relaying the part of the news that could easily have been overwhelming, paralyzing even, something came over her. Something that, by a strange mechanism, allowed her to function at the peak of her abilities, even while her husband was fighting for his life.

From that moment on, her single most important duty was to the kids, and protecting them from the emotional trauma of this crisis would be a lot harder to do if she was consumed by how dire my situation was. So instead, the same thing that had just happened to me, 1,000 miles away, on the baseball field up in Virginia, was happening to her: As things were reaching their worst, something came along to lift the burden.

Only for her, it happened through an unexpected mechanism: humor.

When Jeff Flake said, "He's been hit," Jennifer's mind—jump-started awake by a jolt of confusing news—conjured the image of a cartoon-like commotion, a tornado of bats and balls and helmets flying around, some soft and harmless piece of baseball equipment bouncing comically off my noggin. Now that she had *that* image in her mind, instead of a heart attack or a serious gunshot wound, she felt like a weight had been lifted. *That* she could deal with.

She got back up to her feet, vaguely embarrassed for having been so worried.

"Hit with *what?*" This was all no longer so disturbing.

"He was shot in the hip."

Well, even that sounded pretty innocuous. Seconds ago, she thought I'd had a heart attack. Now she was imagining a little bullet grazing past my leg on the way to a clump of grass.

"Okay, well, can you put him on the phone?"

"They're about to transport him to the hospital."

"He's going to the *hospital*?"

Now she was embarrassed for *me*. A hospital for a little graze?

✤ ✤ ✤

Two minutes later, another call came in; this one from Dave Bailey, who'd just saved the lives of 20 people, maybe more. "Mrs. Tiger, Mrs. Tiger," Dave said, nearly panting Jennifer's Capitol Police call sign, "he's going to be okay! I promise you, he's going to be okay!"

Is *everyone* suddenly a drama queen this morning?

Jen was now fully immersed in a mindset of denial, and it was about to start affecting everything she did. She could hear that Dave was running, but she didn't know he was on duty that morning, so some lever in her brain engaged and conjured an image of him not on the field after a shootout, but at home, out of breath because he was running out of his apartment, running to his car, trying to get to the hospital. Not running because I was seriously wounded, but because he was overreacting. Jen always saw Dave as extraordinarily protective of me, a big brother (albeit one about half my age) who'd be overcome with despair if I stubbed my toe. Jen wasn't worried about me. She was worried about Dave.

"Are *you* okay, Dave?"

"They're taking him to the hospital now. They're taking him by helicopter."

She had to stop herself from laughing. *Helicopter?!* "Why

bring all this attention? This is so overdramatic! Does he really need to go in a helicopter? Isn't that a bit much?"

"They won't let me on the helicopter. Don't worry. I'm going to follow him to the hospital. I'm going to get to him at the hospital."

"Who else got hurt?"

"Well, my ankle is hurt. A bullet ricocheted and hit me. Crystal's down."

"Down?"

In the scenario Jen had conjured, my security detail being shot and incapacitated didn't fit. *Crystal's down? Down where?*

There was a knock at the door.

Jen went to the foyer, kneeled down, and peered through the mail slot. She saw one of her friends.

"What are *you* doing here?"

"You gonna let me in?"

"No, I'm not going to let you in. It'll wake up the kids. If I open the door, the alarm's gonna chime."

And what in the world is everyone freaking out about?!

Jen still hadn't turned on the news. If she'd been watching, she'd have seen what our friends and family were beginning to see—images of me on a stretcher being carried to a helicopter, a baseball field littered with gear, police everywhere.

Soon more friends, having seen the news, started showing up.

My district chief of staff, Charles, arrived, and his brother, Cameron, who had been an aide to me years ago and now held my state House seat.

Then our friends Rick and Karen.

Then the sheriff's deputy chief of operations.

Eventually Jen had no choice but to disengage the alarm and watch our house fill up with all of our overreacting friends.

"Everybody, y'all need to lower your voices! If anybody wakes up the kids, I'm gonna *really* be upset."

By then her phone was ringing nonstop with calls from friends, family, and former staff, so a friend took the phone— then handed it back. "Um, the president is calling you."

"The president of what?"

"What do you mean of what? Of the—of America."

"Why is the president calling?" She took the phone and looked around the room. "What am I supposed to tell the president?"

A woman's voice came over the line, "Can you please hold for the president?"

Jennifer didn't know what the protocol was here. Probably you weren't supposed to say, "No. I won't hold for the president."

The line connected.

"Jennifer! I didn't expect to be woken up on my birthday with this news!"

"Mr. President! It's your birthday?"

"It is."

"Well, happy birthday!" Jen wasn't thinking, *It must be serious if President Trump calling.* She was thinking, *The president's birthday is on Flag Day. Neat!*

"Thanks," the president said. "How is he?"

"I don't know; I haven't been able to talk to him yet."

"Well, he's going to be fine, right? Just got grazed."

And it went on like that for a while, a pleasant, lighthearted conversation, even while up in Washington, D.C., I was hovering right along the border between life and death, the assistant director of trauma was fighting with what looked like a SWAT unit trying to occupy her hospital, and a 15-person trauma team was frantically trying to prep me for surgery but couldn't get a blood pressure reading, which meant my brain probably wasn't getting enough blood. The information about how serious my condition was couldn't get out though, because as helpful as it would have been for the hospital to tell everyone I was dying and they all needed to get the hell out of the way, they couldn't say anything about my condition, unless I consented. I was unconscious, so I couldn't consent to anything, and the only other person who could give them permission was my next of kin. That was Jen, who was, right around then, chatting amiably with the president of the United States about his birthday.

The hospital was caught in a Catch-22. Jen couldn't consent on behalf of her incapacitated husband because she didn't believe her husband was incapacitated. Her husband was fine. He was in stable condition, probably joking with colleagues, eating Jell-O. She'd latched onto the same false early reports President Trump had heard, which meant the false information was actually preventing itself from being corrected.

As frustrating as that was for the hospital, and as problematic as it was for the trauma team and hospital staff, in one way, it was actually helpful. It helped Jen stay in her alternate universe, where she could remain, for the time being, unbothered by what had happened to me, and concentrate instead on what was best for our children. The notion that I was fighting for my life was still nowhere near her consciousness. It wasn't in the same zip code. And if it had been, what would she have done? The reality, though neither of us knew it at the time, was that my life was in the hands of a cast of very special characters performing at the top of their abilities, and the situation was entirely out of our control, hers and mine. As absurd as it seems, her extraordinary ability to build and maintain a screen of denial turned out to be the best possible way for her to protect our kids from the fact that their dad was minutes away from death.

Another phone rang.

This time it was a doctor. Jen put the call on speaker, and they all sat around as the voice on the other end described the situation.

But Jen, in the midst of her shock, wasn't really paying attention.

As the doctor began to speak, she was looking around the room, at all our friends who were listening intently, and found herself distracted by something: how funny all of their expressions were. *Look at their faces!*

She glanced around, from one friend to the next.

Why are their eyes so wide?!

It was like they were all watching a movie, and everybody was reacting to a surprising plot twist Jen had missed.

Jen heard the doctor, without really registering the information, but our friends got the message loud and clear—Jen needed to get up to Washington, *ASAP*.

Ashley, the kids' babysitter, went up to begin laying out clothes for Jen. The rest of them urged her to go up and get ready, and when she finally relented, it was only because she had to pack anyway—for the *next* day's trip, for the baseball game, which she still planned on attending with the kids to cheer me on.

A little later, another call came in; this time, it was the director of the hospital's trauma department, Dr. Jack Sava. They put Sava on speakerphone. As he spoke, Jen was still focused on the next day's trip, making sure she and the kids were packed for the baseball game.

"...in shock," the doctor was saying, "critically injured, lost a lot of blood, probably still bleeding...."

Jen was half-listening

"...given blood to stabilize pressure...seems to be doing okay as long as he's getting blood...."

On the phone, Sava shifted gears; he was asking something. "When are you coming? What time do you get in?"

That, Jen heard.

And now, she was irritated.

Who was this guy? Who did he think he was, trying to control her plans? And by the way, she knew what I'd say if she could just speak to me, could almost *hear* me laughing, saying, *Everything's fine. You're right. Everyone's overreacting; keep an eye on the kids. Don't change anything, don't disrupt their schedule; let them go to camp.*

Perhaps loudest and clearest of all, she could hear my voice telling her, *Don't waste money changing the tickets!* It was frustrating for her, because if she could just get everyone else to hear what she knew I was thinking, they'd leave her alone, they'd understand I was fine, she'd finally get some space, some room to breathe, she'd no longer have to be so anxious about disturbing the kids.

"Doctor," she said, "can you please just put Steve on the phone?"

✦ ✦ ✦

Harrison was the first to wake up. He walked down the stairs to a room full of people.

"Hey baby, good morning!" Jen said, and then, without missing a beat, came up with a plausible, detailed story for why our house was so full of people. "Remember Uncle Greg fixed the sink a couple of weeks ago? Well, it's broken again! He came back to fix it again. Remember Bella's birthday is next week? Miss Melissa came over because she was stopping by to see if Maddie and I wanted to go shopping for Bella's birthday gift. Miss Jamie came over because she brought donuts. How awesome is that? You want donuts?! Ms. Diane and Miss Ashley came to help me pack. Rick and Karen came over because they decided to go to Daddy's baseball game tomorrow, and they're gonna fly with us!"

She had no idea where it was all coming from. It was like someone was whispering these things into her ear and she was just repeating them. All she knew is she felt it was extremely important that our kids stay calm. That was the way to protect them. At first, she just wanted to protect them from fear. But then, from something else.

A colleague of mine managed to get through to Jen and deliver one piece of false but still terrifying information. "Stuff's starting to come in. Steve was the target."

That notion rattled her. Me being the target was hard to reconcile with an errant bullet accidentally grazing past my leg. It didn't change her sense of denial about my condition, but it did introduce an element of *intent* into her thinking. If there were a plot to kill me, why would it stop at just me? Surely there was a team of assassins, planning to kill the entire Scalise family. So now, she had to contend with the feeling that our kids' lives were at risk. Her protective instincts went into overdrive.

She drew the blinds.

She turned off the lights.

She started cracking the door when more friends showed up and made them slip in quickly, in case the assassin was out hiding among the news crew.

She dug in her heels even harder about coming up to see me. If the second assassin wasn't right outside the house, he'd be waiting at the airport. Of course he would be. A crowded place where she and the kids would be vulnerable? He'd be there waiting. Of all the places to go when there's an active conspiracy to kill you and your children, what could be worse than going out in public? To a crowded airport?

What could be worse than going to Washington, D.C.?

Dr. Sava called again. "Do you have a flight yet?" He had urgency in his voice. Why was he so eager for her to risk her children's lives?

Over the phone, Jen could hear Brett in the background, up in D.C., and then Sava asked her for permission to read Brett into what was happening with me. *Yeah, sure, whatever,* but what she really registered was *This man I don't know is still trying to boss me around and put the kids at risk.*

Our friends were pushing hard against her, taking the doctor's side. The people gathered at the house knew how serious things were; they'd heard Sava's calls, they got his message loud and clear. By the time my daughter woke up 30 minutes after Harrison, Jen understood our friends were not going to let it go. They would do whatever it took to get her and the kids up to me, so they could all see me at least one more time if I didn't make it through the day. Our friends would not shut up until she was on a plane and on her way to me. Finally, reluctantly, she relented; if only so she could have a few moments of quiet.

Maddie padded down the stairs and saw all our friends in the house. "What's going on?"

Jen collected herself, repeated the backstories she'd made up for Harrison about each person, then came up with a way of breaking the news that the plans had all changed. "Hey guess what? We're going to go up to D.C. a day early!"

"What about camp?"

Maddie looked worried; she understood this must be some kind of an emergency.

Out of nowhere, Jen came up with a way of allaying those fears. She used the information she'd learned from the phone call with the president.

"Well, listen to how cool this is. Today is Donald Trump's birthday. He invited Mommy and Daddy to his birthday party! We can't say no. We can't tell the president no, can we?"

It was an inspired bit of improvisation, and it worked, just enough. I think Madison always sensed something was going on, but I also think she trusted that if Mom was changing the plans a little, there must be a good reason. I think Maddie sensed it was time to cooperate.

So finally, the kids listening to their mom, and their mom

listening to the crowd in the house, they found themselves packed into a plane with several of our friends, approaching Reagan National Airport in Washington, while Jen tried to quiet her sense of foreboding about an assassin waiting for her and the kids at the airport.

The SUV I usually rode in was now a shredded heap of broken glass, flat tires, and perforated side paneling over at the baseball field, surrounded by crime scene tape, about to be taken to FBI impound as evidence, so they were picked up at the airport in my advance vehicle, a big Ford Expedition, that's usually used to scout a location before I get there.

As they sat in the Expedition on the way to the hotel, Jen could almost *feel* our friends in the SUV wondering how she was going to break the news to Maddie and Harrison. She was beginning to accept, intellectually at least, that things were bad, although she was still more focused on what she could do to protect the kids. She knew eventually she'd have to tell them I wasn't doing well, and even then, in the car, she could sense questions swirling around in our friends' minds.

What are you going to say when he doesn't come home tonight?
She didn't know.

She just knew this wasn't the time.

But she also knew that the more time that passed without her telling them, the more likely it was they'd find out by accident. On TV, on the radio, overhearing something on a phone. Any of those scenarios would be much worse. She had no good options. Once Jen arrived in the hotel lobby with the kids, she thought of the TVs in the hotel room. As far as she knew, the shooting could be all over the news. "I just need to run up and unplug—"

"It's already taken care of."

Ellen Gosnell, my scheduler, and Stephanie Belk, the political coordinator for my Leadership Fund, had taken it upon themselves to meet Jen and the kids at the hotel, because they knew Jen would need to leave as soon as she could for the hospital and might need some help looking after the kids. They'd already thought of the fact that Jen might not want the kids hearing what happened quite yet.

When the kids got to the room, they didn't even ask why none of the TVs worked. They were just excited to play with their cool older friends.

"Okay," Jen said. "It's time for me to go meet Daddy for the party!"

Before leaving, she had one last thought: What if the kids waited up for us? If they thought I was coming home from a party, they'd wait up all night. They'd done it before, fighting to keep their eyes open into the small hours, just so they could wish Daddy goodnight.

Jen pulled our friends Karen and Rick over to the corner. "Would you mind if they slept in your room tonight?"

Karen gave her a knowing nod. She turned to Maddie and Harrison. "Hey kids!" she said, "Do y'all want to do a sleepover in our room?!"

No matter what the circumstances, few things are more exciting to kids than sleepovers. Especially sleepovers in hotel rooms.

Jen was ready to come see me.

7:52 AM

TRAUMA BAY 2

Over the baseball field, the chopper banked north and raced over the Potomac, as a dedicated phone line began ringing in the Medical Shock Trauma Acute Resuscitation unit, or Med-STAR, at the MedStar Washington Hospital Center.

A nurse answered, took down the information, then picked up a separate phone that connects to the hospital's main communications center, and dictated a short message.

The communications center, in turn, sent a page to every member of the trauma team.

At almost the exact same moment that pagers started buzzing on hips in the hospital, a call went over the overhead public address system:

CODE YELLOW TO MEDSTAR! FIVE
MINUTES BY HELICOPTER!

Every member of the trauma team knows what to do when a page like that comes through. They rush to the trauma bay—they run if they're far away—so they can prep for whatever's incoming. They flip on lights, bring up warm blankets, bring blood up from the lab, take their positions, and do all of it with extraordinary speed. A 10- or sometimes 15-person team leaves whatever they were just doing and converges on the trauma bay to get everything set up.

Susan Kennedy, a nurse and the hospital's assistant director of trauma, makes sure it all happens in just a matter of minutes.

But that day was a little different.

The call from the helicopter came at a special moment in the daily rhythm of the hospital's trauma unit, and the timing turned out to be another small miracle.

Every morning, just after the doctors and nurses arrive, and just before the overnight team leaves, there's a short period of time during which they all overlap. During that period, the two teams meet so they can make sure they're on the same page about the patients under their care. The night team tells the day team how the night went, what's going on with each patient, who to keep an eye on, who's ready to be discharged, and who took a turn for the worse. These "pass on rounds" take just a few minutes, but they're minutes during which both teams are gathered in a conference room, right next to the trauma unit. The call from the chopper came in at exactly that moment of overlap.

Not only was the team already in position, near the trauma bay—there were also twice as many people ready to respond. Had the call come a moment later, the night team would have left already. Had it come a moment earlier, the day team wouldn't have been there yet. The shock trauma unit had twice the staff it would have had if that call had come in at almost literally any other moment.

And that turned out to be a blessing, because when the helicopter landed, I was not on it.

✣ ✣ ✣

The pilot knew even before he landed with Special Agent Griner that he was going to turn around and go back to the field just as soon as he could.

He knew that whatever was happening on the ground, it was bad, and from the air, above the field, as he lifted off, it was obvious no one was going to be able to move around very quickly down there. The field had quickly been designated a crime scene, the basketball court wrapped in yellow caution tape and stuffed with addled congressmen still in their baseball gear. The streets were gridlocked, some of them deliberately shut down by police, some just clogged by emergency responders trying to get there to help. The pilot knew that if anyone else was seriously wounded, they'd need a helicopter to get to a hospital with any speed.

He brought the bird down onto the trauma center's helipad and left the rotors spinning while the flight medic ran out with Crystal and gave what may well have been the world's fastest patient handoff. The intake nurse happened to be one of the most experienced in the hospital and understood what was happening. She didn't ask the flight medic to linger. Where usually there's an elaborate handoff—the helicopter crew giving the patient's medical history, what steps have already been taken, what allergies the patient has—on that day, the nurse on duty said, in effect, "We got this. Get the hell outta here."

They wheeled Crystal into Trauma Bay 1, and even before she was inside, the chopper was up above the hospital, banking south, back toward Virginia, back toward me.

Then, in what felt like the blink of an eye, it returned.

It was like time had skipped forward a beat.

The chopper dropped Griner off a little before 8:00 AM. It dropped me off a little after 8:00 AM.

Even in retrospect, it still doesn't actually seem possible. In that time, just a few minutes, the pilot flew from northwest Washington, D.C., down past the Washington Mall, past the Washington Monument, past the Pentagon and Reagan National Airport, to the park in Alexandria, and then did that trip in reverse.

He had to take off and land twice, as well as load and unload two patients.

The pilot later said, "I flew that bird like I stole it," and, certainly, he pushed the helicopter as fast as it could go. It also helped that the Park Police beat other helicopters to the scene, because the Park Police don't have to worry about flying through restricted airspace, since they're the ones restricting it.

Both of those things make sense.

I don't think either totally explains it.

❖ ❖ ❖

From the moment they wheeled me into Trauma Bay 2, the team knew I was in trouble. Susan Kennedy didn't need to hook me up to instruments to know I was on the brink.

My skin was pallid, gray, and dead looking. My cognitive function was in rapid decline. My blood pressure had plummeted, and I was in hemorrhagic shock. I'd lost more than a fifth of the fluid in my body already. I'd lost so much blood that my veins were deflating. My heart rate was spiking because my heart was trying to pump a smaller amount of blood up to my brain, but it wasn't working. My brain still wasn't getting enough blood. I was basically unconscious already. I was mumbling, but registering nothing. My body temperature had plummeted. I was going into a death spiral, a cycle of functions shutting down, each critical system failure compounding another. As I lost blood, my body got colder. As my body got colder, my cells stopped working right. As my cells stopped working right, my blood stopped clotting. As my blood stopped clotting, I lost blood faster. As I lost blood faster, my body temperature dropped even faster, which meant my blood clotted even less effectively, and on and on the spiral went.

The team surrounded me and got to work. Kennedy's team had the whole process down to a well-choreographed dance, each person with his or her own predetermined role and a predetermined place at the table, based on what they were supposed to be doing: one nurse on the side of the bed starting a new IV; the medical student running to get the sonogram machine in order to do an ultrasound on my abdomen and confirm internal bleeding; the emergency medicine staff on hand to secure an airway in case I stopped breathing; Dr. Anthony Shiflett, the surgeon running the resuscitation, at the head of the bed just off to my right, so that if I woke up, he could talk to me.

At that point, I had no idea what was going on, and I have no memory of it now. I wasn't forming complete sentences. I wasn't making sense.

They checked the IVs and put in new ones because it was going to get harder and harder to establish and maintain lines to get fluid into my body. As veins flattened out, it was harder to find them and to get needles in without pushing all the way through the other side of the vein, dumping fluid into tissue instead of my bloodstream.

The veins that were easy to see wouldn't work. The raised veins on the top of my hands were accessible, but they're small and thin, and if you put too much pressure on them they blow apart. And I needed a lot of fluid. It was another Catch-22: To inflate the veins, you need to increase blood pressure. To increase blood pressure, you need the veins to be inflated, so you can get an IV in. Having good IV lines was going to be critical, because they were going to need to start pushing blood into me with a huge amount of speed and pressure if I was going to have a chance at surviving.

✤ ✤ ✤

They cut off the rest of my clothes and rolled me over to double check that someone along the way hadn't missed other wounds.

They ran x-rays. They saw that my femur was fractured and, more importantly, that my pelvis was shattered. When surgeons see a fractured femur, they're thinking about whether the person will walk again. When they see a shattered pelvis, they're thinking about whether the person will survive. It's a complicated, busy part of the body with lots of things that can bleed. And on the x-ray, they could see hundreds of pieces of shrapnel.

They ran the sonogram to see if I had fluid in my abdomen and confirmed that I did. There was heavy internal bleeding, though it wasn't clear where all of it was coming from. They could see pools of blood, but not any one source of blood; there seemed to be *many* sources. It wasn't as if I had a cut inside me somewhere; it was as if I was bleeding from dozens of places, maybe more. Because the bullet hit bone and all of it fragmented, I'd had, in effect, hundreds of pieces of shrapnel bouncing around inside my pelvis and abdominal cavity, cutting through blood vessels and organs. It wasn't immediately obvious how they were going to be able to stop all of the bleeding. What they knew was that I'd already lost way too much blood. If they were going to have any hope of saving me, they needed to get a lot of blood back into me very quickly to keep me alive long enough for them to figure out what to do next.

They called down to the hospital's blood bank. "We're enacting the MTP."

In the blood bank, a tech took the call. "Got it. Blood bank enacting Massive Transfusion Protocol."

With that, the blood bank ground to a halt.

All other orders were put on hold.

All the bank's resources were redirected toward one goal: keeping that one patient up in Trauma Bay 2 alive.

First, they sent a Playmate cooler full of blood up to the trauma bay.

Then they thawed blood plasma, mixed the blood components, made more blood bags, packed another cooler, and ran that one up to me.

Then another.

And another.

The blood bank continued like that, continuously sending

blood in a new cooler every 15 minutes, on autopilot, with no plan to stop unless explicitly ordered to.

Without the MTP, I would have died there on the table. Because blood was coming up constantly and, save for the first call, no one even had to ask for it, Dr. Shiflett and the trauma team were given just a little bit of extra time to figure out what to do next. The Massive Transfusion Protocol is a system perfected in combat hospitals by forward deployed doctors like Brad Wenstrup, and it saves lives both by saving time and by buying it. Not only does it save doctors from having to constantly order more blood, but also it saves them from having to talk to the lab through the specific mixture of blood they want. That had already been figured out, the right mixture optimized through the hard lessons of combat. Where soldiers have died, other people have benefitted. Countless soldiers injured or killed while serving this country, and every doctor and nurse who treated them, have helped give trauma patients extra time. As does everyone who gives blood. I had 20 units of blood transfused into my body. I had the blood of almost three whole people put into me.

They couldn't just put the blood directly into me, though, because to preserve blood, they have to chill it. Already my body temperature was plummeting. Pumping cold blood into an already cold body would do as much damage as it did good, so even though I was bleeding out, they warmed the blood in a special machine before transfusing it, and when they transfused it, they didn't just hang it on a bag and let it drip in; the machine actually squeezed the blood into my body. They had to force the blood in. They couldn't just let gravity do the work. I didn't have time.

✦ ✦ ✦

On her way into work earlier that morning, Susan Kennedy's phone had buzzed with a news alert about a shooting in Virginia. She was perhaps the only person in the greater Washington region whose response was excitement. Kennedy's first thought was, *Maybe we'll get some penetrating trauma today!*

For her, a good day at work is getting to see a gnarly injury and then getting to see it fixed.

If that sounds ghoulish, it's just that Kennedy's a trauma nurse, through and through. She oversees the trauma unit, but what animates her, in equal measure, is helping people and getting the adrenaline rush of looking at a broken thing that needs to be fixed urgently and figuring out how to fix it. Back when she was just starting out and choosing where to take her first job as a nurse, she chose MedStar Washington Hospital Center over Jefferson University Hospital in Philadelphia, even though Philadelphia is her hometown, because at the time Jefferson didn't have its own helicopter. MedStar Washington Hospital Center has three helicopters running 24/7 and a fourth running during the day. Helicopters are sexier; helicopters mean gnarlier injuries. It was no contest.

Some people run toward danger rather than away from it because of courage and, sometimes, because of curiosity. With Kennedy, it's a little of both. On 9/11, after a plane struck the Pentagon, the hospital dispatched a helicopter to the scene and got two patients out before the air space was shut down. There's a photo Kennedy has framed in her office of their helicopter, hovering above the giant gash through the E and D rings of the Pentagon, set against a sky gone brown from smoke. She was proud to be part of a team that had saved even those two people amid that danger, chaos, and tragedy; proud enough to make it the image that hangs above her whenever she sits in her office. She's one of those people, like some fighter pilots or war correspondents, whose professions align their thrill-seeking, adrenaline junkie personality with a sense of duty.

So on that day in June, Kennedy was not intimidated, unprepared, or surprised when the Park Service helicopter landed outside the trauma bay with a major trauma victim. She was excited. She was ready. She'd just about seen it all.

What *did* surprise her, what she *hadn't* seen before, was what happened about 10 minutes after they wheeled me off that chopper: Two dozen members of what looked like a commando unit came running up the ambulance ramp, entered the trauma bay, and surrounded it.

It felt like an armed paramilitary invasion, as if Kennedy and the other doctors and nurses gathered around me were cabinet members about to be deposed in a violent coup.

For a moment, Kennedy was stunned. *What the*—but she had no time. She had a mission, and whoever these people were, what mattered was that they were in the way.

"No, no, *no!* We're providing care here! You guys need to— *guys!* Silence your radios and get out of our faces!" It sounded to Kennedy like each soldier, or whatever they were, was carrying six different communication devices, all of them buzzing and beeping at the same time. She'd been, on some level, conscious of the fact that a member of Congress may have been hurt, she'd heard but dismissed the "Congress" part of the news reports, because that wasn't what was interesting to her. What was interesting to her was the prospect of trauma victims at her hospital. Now, the task at hand was not trying to save a congressman; it was trying to save a human being. She wasn't thinking about whether the body in shock bleeding out in her trauma bay was a billionaire philanthropist or a convicted murderer. She and everyone else around the table were focused on saving me, regardless of who I was. My identity wasn't at all relevant.

Until, suddenly, it was. The trauma team found themselves in the middle of what felt like a hostile military occupation of their trauma bay, and Kennedy looked at the patient on table—at me. *Who the hell* is *this guy?*

These SWAT guys were in the way. She was, for the first time in a while, worried, which she's not accustomed to being. She's not the kind of person who's easily scared or intimidated. She's the kind of person who usually sees a devastating mass-casualty multicar accident as an opportunity for professional growth.

She was worried, though, for the same reason firefighter and paramedic Richard Krimmer had been worried half an hour before. Like the back of the ambulance, the trauma bay is very carefully laid out to maximize the efficiency of the team working inside it. It's designed to provide just enough space for each of them, while still allowing each of them easy reach to the instruments they need. They practice their choreography in that space. "Trauma is a team sport," Kennedy likes to say, and the space is laid out specifically to allow interaction among teammates. Each bay is wide enough that a gurney can be wheeled in with doctors and nurses and techs on the side—but not patient, doctors, nurses, techs, *and* armed men in full tactical gear.

The situation was becoming increasingly hectic. It was getting louder and louder. As the doctors and nurses tried to work, they were having a harder and harder time hearing each other. The tension of trying to save my life was compounded by the noise and commotion of the armed men, and soon it became clear that it wasn't *just* that one unit of armed men; they'd been trailed by uniformed Capitol Police and plain-clothes officers filing into the halls, trying (and generally failing) to blend in while they secured entrances and exits.

Kennedy was concerned about her patient and concerned for her team. The commandos were in the way. She needed to do something about it. They were heavily armed, but, well, the patient comes first. So she puffed out her chest, and armed with nothing but her conviction that she needed to take control of the situation, Susan Kennedy turned around and stared down an entire unit of men holding semi-automatic rifles.

Here, again, there was a convergence of the people trying to save my life and the people trying to protect it.

✣ ✣ ✣

At around that time, the hospital's media relations director, So Yung Pak, was running around trying to figure out what was going on. Once reporters learned I was in the hospital, they began reporting I was in "stable condition." Pak couldn't figure out where that idea had come from. Certainly no one at the hospital would have said that, but now the lack of information was confounding to reporters and my friends alike: If I was in stable condition, why was the hospital being so evasive about me?

Pak, like the doctors and nurses, felt she couldn't correct

the misinformation without my consent, and I couldn't give consent. I was crashing. I was unconscious. I couldn't very well consent to anything. I wasn't in "stable condition." I was dying.

By the time the SWAT-type guys showed up, Pak and Susan Kennedy had a decent idea I was some kind of public figure, but they still didn't know anything for sure. Pak was in a position that made it impossible to do her job, and Susan Kennedy, even as she was overseeing a unit treating a crashing patient, saw that her friend's hands were effectively tied. For Kennedy, the "team sport" instinct kicked in, and as she turned to face down the guerilla unit that had run up on the trauma bay, she thought, *Maybe they can also help us here.*

"Hey. *HEY!* What are you doing here? Why are you here?"

"Sorry ma'am, we can't tell you."

Kennedy picked one of them out and got in his face. "I need to know. Is this a person of interest? I need to know, and I need to know *now.*"

"I'm sorry. I can't tell you."

The hospital and the men were both committed to confidentiality, two commitments coming into direct conflict.

"Then you get your people out of here." She tried to make it sound like she'd somehow actually be able to enforce that threat.

"We need to be here to secure the building. Is he doing okay?"

"Do you want me to save his life, or do you want to stand here and talk about it?"

"Well, we're not...sorry, we can't...I mean, we're not leaving."

"I need to know. I need to manage the situation, so you've got to fess up and tell me."

Finally, reluctantly, he said, "Yes."

"Okay. Your immediate team can stay."

"Fine."

That scaled the number of GI Joes down to 10.

"Everybody else takes 10 giant steps back and silences their radios."

Soon Cedric showed up from the Democrats' practice, still in his baseball uniform—he got to the hospital even before members of my own party—then my staff got there, then more of my colleagues from Congress. Kennedy and Pak conferred again. "What are we going to do with these guys?"

The guys closest to me in the world were there, thinking they'd pop into a room to laugh and sign a cast. Kennedy couldn't even tell them they might never see me again. Someone told her the White House was calling.

The White House?

She called Pak. "The White House is calling me. Is this a hoax? What am I supposed to do?"

"Why are they calling?"

"They want a status. The White House wants a status on the patient, but I can't tell them anything."

Even giving the president of the United States an update on my status would be a violation of my privacy, an unauthorized disclosure of medical information, and they weren't willing to do that, even though they still didn't even know who I was.

In the span of half an hour, Kennedy had to confront an

armed tactical police unit, US congressmen, and the president of the United States.

Even for her, it was becoming an extraordinary day.

✣ ✣ ✣

Back in Trauma Bay 2, I was crashing, but I had signs of life. I had a heart rate, though it was way too fast. I was in shock, so my heart was pumping furiously, much faster than it's supposed to, desperately trying to get the little blood I had to my brain.

Dr. Shiflett and the trauma team had a critical decision to make. They didn't have much time; a few moments more and I'd be gone. They needed to get me into surgery immediately and to begin an aggressive approach to stop the internal bleeding. They could begin surgery in the trauma bay, but it's easier to do it in an operating room, where there's more equipment and space for more doctors and nurses. The operating room, the OR, was a minute or two away, though, so they had to decide whether to start surgery right then or make the trip.

Was it worth taking on the risk of a move if it increased my odds of survival at the other end of it?

Shiflett decided to do it. He thought I could survive that minute trip, if not much more, and he knew he had one of the finest trauma surgeons down there ready to help, if he could get me to the OR alive. Shiflett made the call to move. He left the table to send a text to Dr. Jack Sava, director of the trauma department, to tell him I was in trouble and they were bringing me to the OR. Meanwhile, Susan Kennedy turned around to negotiate with the Rambo guys.

"We're moving him."

One of the men said something into a radio.

Quietly, without even having to communicate, the team formed a ring around Kennedy's team, which, in turn, formed a ring around me, and everyone started moving—started *running*—down the hall. One of the junior members of the team ran alongside me with a hand pressed down on the wound, to keep the pressure on, even as we ran.

As we barreled down the hall, Kennedy suddenly realized they were about to run into a problem: We couldn't all fit in the elevator. It's big enough for a gurney and the medical team, but not 20 armed men in tactical gear. There wasn't time to waste having a discussion about it in front of the elevator. "You five," she yelled as they ran, "you come with me!"

She kicked into a higher gear, running faster than the medical team and the gurney, splitting off and leading a group of the armed men to a back way, to a door that opened into a stairwell. They took the stairs two at a time, while the medical team, the rest of the commando unit, and I went down on the elevator.

The whole massive team came back together one floor down.

The commando unit then divided once again, a unit of five running in front of the gurney, a unit on each side of the gurney, and a unit of five running behind, everyone barreling down the hall toward the operating room. The team flew past even *more* new people who'd filed into the hospital; these were plainclothes officers who looked to Kennedy like they were about to go fishing, men wearing Hawaiian shirts, like they were trying to look casual, trying to blend in, even as they spoke into coiled plastic earpieces.

❖ ❖ ❖

Once in the operating room, they couldn't find my blood pressure. Dr. Sava determined I was at imminent risk of death. He wouldn't have operated if he thought I had *no* chance—it'd be unethical to render futile care—but he wasn't making any promises.

At that point, the most optimistic he could bring himself to feel was that I had a chance.

If everything went perfectly, if he and his team didn't make even a *single* mistake, I at least had a chance.

8:20 AM

JACK SAVA, M.D.

The first time Jack Sava saw somebody die was in medical school. He'd just been talking to a woman, and a moment later, she was having a heart attack.

There was a team around her, but it was the doctor coming in to run the resuscitation who left a lifelong impression on Sava.

Something in the way he spoke, even the way he looked, his facial expressions—it hypnotized the team. A moment before, it had been frantic, frenetic, and then this doctor came in and everyone was aligned, working together, calm. The way the doctor pronounced words was so calm and exaggerated it seemed almost medicated, almost musical. The way he asked for this tool, for that medicine; each word seemed to carry within it a sedative effect.

The experience imprinted on Sava. The trauma of seeing someone die never left him, but mixed in with that memory was the doctor taking such total control of a team that he actually managed to alter how each member felt stress. Sava walked out of the hospital that day thinking not quite *Someday I'll be like him*, but *Someday I'll know how he did that*. Sava had been a philosophy major in college, so he had a hard time letting questions go. He treated them, no matter how esoteric they seemed, like machines to take apart and look at from different angles.

As he progressed through medical school, then went on to

residency and fellowship, the idea stuck with him: That fear and stress were things that could be controlled. And that, therefore, there must be ways to reduce the incidence of mistakes people make when they're frightened or stressed.

The question was, *How?*

In his spare time, Sava read books about fear and stress, trying to understand exactly what fear actually was and how it worked, hunting to find things he could incorporate into his work as a surgeon.

He started picking up tidbits. A former Navy SEAL asked him to consult on a new tourniquet he was developing and explained to Sava where the design philosophy had come from. "In my line of work," the former SEAL said, "we have a saying that we don't want to carry any device we can't use while wearing the boxing gloves of fear."

The very next day, Sava was called to respond to a "code blue airway," which is just about the most emergent thing that can happen in a hospital. It means someone's airway is blocked. Someone wasn't breathing. The patient had seconds to live. Sava rushed to respond and had just seconds to cut into the patient's neck to create an airway. He grabbed a scalpel, and he noticed—as the patient beside him struggled to breathe—how idiotic it was that the scalpel came disassembled, in a tiny foil package that was about as hard to open as a pack of airplane peanuts. After fussing with the package, he had to remove the safety blade, and then to get the scalpel assembled and ready to use, he had to perform a whole series of fine motor skill tasks that would have been difficult to execute had he been sitting in a spa with scented candles and harp music playing, let alone in a hospital with a patient's eyes bulging, terrified family members screaming, and the boxing gloves of fear hobbling his fingers.

After that, Sava was sure of it: Real, tangible things could increase or decrease the likelihood of mistakes doctors make under pressure.

Sava began doing research. He developed a series of questions to ask his peers in the surgery field. "What are the qualities that help you manage stress? How can you tell when you're getting stressed?"

He did not receive a very warm reception. Frustrated colleagues started calling him.

"Jack, c'mon, what is this?"

"This is a waste of time!"

"You owe me a case of beer!"

"This is dumb! You've either got it or you don't! You know that."

The world of trauma surgery, it turned out, wasn't exactly a Kumbaya crowd eager to sit around a campfire and talk about feelings. To Sava, they all seemed to think they were too cool, that they'd all been endowed with an unteachable, innate poise. They saw themselves as just preternaturally cool under pressure. They saw themselves as akin to fighter pilots, Navy SEALs, elite athletes, or concert musicians.

Then Sava's hospital just happened to hire a group of former fighter pilots, Navy SEALs, elite athletes, and concert musicians.

They were all members of a consulting company that hospital administrators brought in to leverage experience from their varied fields into improving the hospital's efficiency.

Sava saw his chance. When the consultants came to ask him questions, he turned the tables and grilled them on the fields they'd come from.

"Do you guys study stress?"

"How do you handle fear?"

"Do you have ways to keep a team from making mistakes under pressure?"

He found that the most elite branches of the military looked at stress the way he did—not as an inevitable impairment, but as a phenomenon to understand. They saw fear and stress as problems as real as gunshot wounds, if much harder to find and treat. They told Sava about tools the military was developing to try and get a grasp on stress, like arm bands that use physiological proxies to measure fear and stress. They told him how they believed that the future of America's elite special forces would be defined as much by a better ability to understand fear and control its effect on performance as it would be by high-tech weapons.

Sava went back to his colleagues in the surgery field. "Okay, I'll get you your case of beer, but let me ask you this: Do you think you're too cool for fighter pilots and Navy SEALs? That's not a club you want to be associated with? Because they're studying this stuff too."

✤ ✤ ✤

Sava started borrowing techniques, and as he moved up in his field, he incorporated them into his work as a trauma surgeon. He started running new trainees through specially designed exercises, to teach them how to handle themselves in high-level trauma surgery. He designed a "model of communication" less prone to error; he was literally re-teaching trainees how to talk. His team became a live-action sociology experiment, in which no proposal for addressing the boxing gloves of fear was too outlandish. Sava had his team start wearing colored bouffant hats, with each color representing the wearer's role during a high-level trauma surgery.

He instituted a protocol whereby all the people in the operating room had to announce their own names and their roles during the resuscitation. People who'd known each other for decades were introducing themselves to one another. At first it felt extremely awkward, and even funny, but like the colored hats, it helped prevent a phenomenon that becomes increasingly probable the more critical a situation is and the more doctors and nurses around the table there are: It becomes very easy to make the justified, well-reasoned, and even polite but wrong assumption that someone else is handling a critical task. As a result, that task never gets done. An anesthesiologist doesn't want to step on the lead surgeon's toes, so the anesthesiologist leaves the task of ordering a blood transfusion to the lead surgeon, who is, in turn, deferring to the anesthesiologist whose specialties include blood, and amid the chaos, no one calls the blood bank until it's too late.

At a Trauma Level 1 center like MedSTAR, there are many doctors highly qualified in multiple areas, which means many of them can perform many different roles. But respecting your colleague's capabilities, or seniority, can be fatal.

So Sava makes people go through an exercise that feels

like introducing yourself to the person you had lunch with yesterday in order to clarify precisely what your task for the next 30 minutes is going to be.

When the surgery begins, Sava's insistence on stating the obvious continues. He calls this having a "shared mental model" built into the "communication expectation." In plain English, it means that basically, you're not allowed to keep their thoughts to themselves. No one's allowed to think something and then decide it's too obvious or too foolish to share. If one member of the team observes the patient is going into shock, she says, "He's going into shock."

Sava insists on this because when someone's about to die, there's no shortage of problems to fix and no shortage of seemingly obvious "most important problems." That makes it easy for everyone to assume they're all working toward the same goal. But there's also no shortage of ways in which addressing one problem can distract from another. Or even make it worse. If you observe the person is dying of blood loss, you announce it, even if it seems obvious; you don't assume that just because there's blood everywhere everyone's working to stop the bleeding. If a patient has stopped breathing, you don't just assume everyone else has seen and heard the beeping monitors.

Sava incorporated a lesson he learned from aviation. After a plane crashes, it often comes out that someone knew about the problem before the plane crashed. Someone in the control tower, or someone in the cockpit, saw a problem but was intimidated, thought it was stupid, assumed it was obvious, and decided not to say anything. Sava makes sure the most junior person around the table is made to feel he or she is an intelligent being, whose observations are welcomed, even by the most senior, busy surgeon there.

Sava himself tries to behave in a way that makes people all around him—but especially those at the bottom of the power hierarchy—feel they can speak their minds without some elder statesman snapping, "Are *you* trying to tell *me* how to do my job?"

And while he was looking at aviation, Sava borrowed another mode of communication, "closed loop communication." If Sava asks, "Can I have a unit of blood and a surgical clamp?" The response should not be, "Sure, no problem." But, instead, "Getting you one unit of blood and a surgical clamp." The "closed loop" reduces the chances of mistakes that happen when multiple people are asking and responding to multiple questions in a frenetic environment. In those high-pressure situations, it's easy for a surgeon's request to go unheard. Even worse, a surgeon can ask a question and hear a "Yeah" he thinks was meant for him, but was really in response to a different request. The unit of blood and the surgical clamp never come.

"Think of Chinese restaurants," Sava tells new team members. "They don't let you off the phone until they've repeated your whole order back to you."

All of this takes extra time, and time itself is another thing Sava works on.

In high-level trauma emergencies, when lives hang in the balance, you don't have a lot of time. But you usually have just a little more time than you think you do. It's another thing Sava learned with the help of his new fighter pilot and special forces friends—that when you're experiencing fear or stress, your

perce...   s distorted. Sava
                                        ake decisions in
                                        afford to stop,
                                        often have four
                                        ed to make in
                                        ive seconds is
                                        n one.
                                        hey're con-
s   keep their
v   live-action
so   ople are in
the   wants to
inc_   __ begin to talk over one
ano_   __ppens in a restaurant's kitchen, it happens at a
party, it happens in your living room at Thanksgiving. Before
you know it, people are almost shouting, and no one remembers exactly why the shouting started.

With a patient on the brink of death, the volume can get
out of hand quickly, fuel stress, and drown out critical information exchange, especially when you add something unexpected to the mix.

Like a dozen men and women with semi-automatic rifles
waving around and radios going off, charging into your hospital.

✛ ✛ ✛

At around 8:20 AM, Dr. Sava received a text message from
his partner, Dr. Anthony Shiflett: "He looks bad, heading to
the OR."

Back up in the trauma bay, as Susan Kennedy coordinated

a phalanx of men and women sprinting down the hall with me on the gurney, Sava hustled to the operating room to meet them. He scrubbed in, as a mass of people converged from different parts of the hospital.

Sava took one look and thought I was at imminent risk of death. I didn't have a blood pressure anyone could measure. Brad's tourniquet had already been removed, but Sava could tell right away that without that tourniquet, I would have been dead before getting to the hospital. Brad had given me a chance. It wasn't a great chance. But it was a chance.

Sava decided to suspend the "role clarity" introductions. There wasn't time.

They were a group of people with overlapping expertise ready to start a complex operation with many moving parts, the risk of a mix-up was high, and with my condition so dire, even just one mistake would probably mean the difference between life and death. Still, Sava decided he had no choice but to hope that the "shared communication model" would prevail and bring down the chance of mistakes, just because they'd rehearsed it for so long, and in the interest of speed, he'd take on the task of clarifying roles himself.

He decided he didn't want to think about getting blood into me and wanted to make sure no one mistakenly deferred to him about it. "Anesthesia," he said, "you're in charge of fluids and blood. I'm not even going to think about that."

"Okay. Anesthesia's in charge of fluids and blood."

He wanted to make sure they didn't keep silent about blood pressure; it'd be important for him to know how I was doing. "Let me know if anything changes up there, and I'll do the same from here."

He wanted to make sure the most junior person around the table wouldn't be intimidated if he or she saw a problem no one else saw, so Sava immediately broke down the barriers of hierarchy. He looked at the young doctor who'd come running into the room with a hand on the bullet wound and said, "I want you to keep holding that. If you notice anything, if it seems like it's bleeding around your fingers, anything, please feel free to let me know."

The junior members had all just been reminded their input was invited.

He told everyone around the table, "I'll keep you informed about whether or not we're seeing new bleeding and how things are coming along."

And then he got to work.

Sava made a big incision down the middle of my abdomen, inserted metal retractors to pull edges away, and opened me up. He started packing the opening full of cotton sponges to absorb some of the blood and to clear his view.

He'd effectively just popped the hood. What he saw was bad. The bullet fragments had covered a lot of territory in there; a destructive shrapnel wave had rolled from one side of me to the other, and just about everything in its path had been torn apart, damaged, or destroyed. He was looking for where, exactly, the blood was coming from, but it seemed to be coming from just about everywhere. *Everywhere* was bleeding.

The sponges slowed the bleeding just a little, and since they'd had the Massive Transfusion Protocol under way during the mad dash from the trauma bay, I now registered a blood pressure, but it started to yo-yo as Sava worked.

One by one, he found things that were bleeding and casually described each one, helping to keep the team calm as he sewed things shut. He saw how many organs were damaged, fixed the ones he could, and found temporary solutions for the ones that would need further surgery.

He pulled damaged and dead tissue away, connected things that had been severed, and closed up holes where he could find them.

With the blood bank now solely focused on getting blood to the anesthesia team, and the anesthesia team focused on getting blood into my body, anesthesia and Sava were at risk of working at cross-purposes. Each time Sava found a bleeding artery or organ and stopped the bleed, he was pushing my blood pressure back up. It was like filling up a water balloon and then squeezing off part of it—that pressure has to go somewhere.

Each time he saw a bleeder, before he stopped it, he told anesthesia exactly what he was about to do, so they wouldn't be given a false sense of security by a sudden improvement in blood pressure and wouldn't get too excited that I was bouncing back.

Meanwhile, even though I was still bleeding badly, if the anesthesia team jacked up the blood pressure too fast, it could cause something Sava had already sewn shut to burst open again. They were squeezing fluids into a container whose volume was shrinking as Sava worked. Things could burst; things could break.

On the other hand, if Sava and the anesthesia team were perfectly coordinated, they could actually use low blood pressure to their advantage. I could begin to clot off some of my own bleeding *because* the pressure was so low, just like how, in a slow-moving river, it's easier for debris and branches to get stuck, to catch and build up, and, eventually, to stop the current.

So Jack Sava slowed himself. He slowed his speaking. He told himself he had at least a *bit* more time than he felt he had. He used the tone and the speed of his voice to convey calm. He kept his voice low, so that no one would have to speak loudly even if they had something urgent to say.

He asked the intern, the most junior member of the team, what he was seeing and thinking.

He recited every step he took, even the obvious ones.

In short, he channeled the doctor from that day in medical school, speaking in a calm, exaggerated manner. He hoped that now, all these years later, he'd answered the question, he'd cracked the code of how to limit mistakes in pressurized environments, and he hoped he would be able to have even half the impact on his team as that doctor had all those years ago.

When Sava or one of the other doctors wasn't sure what accounted for a change in blood pressure, they just asked.

"Is that you, or was that me?"

"Sorry, think that was me," Sava said, "just stopped a big one."

Sava was finding and sealing one big bleed after another, but he started to feel he wasn't having enough success. Without raising his voice, he communicated his thoughts to the others around the table. He asked anesthesia, "What are you guys seeing? Do you think we've got a good chance at making it to IR right now?"

Me, about 10 years old, at a 4th of July parade in Metairie, LA. (Author's collection)

My mother, Carol, and me at a fraternity event at Louisiana State University in 1986. (Author's collection)

Jennifer and me on our wedding day outside the St. Louis Cathedral in New Orleans, March 19, 2005. (Author's collection)

Running for the Louisiana State Senate, with my former aide Cameron Henry, who was running for my State House seat in November 2007. (Author's collection)

Me and 10-month-old Madison at the Louisiana State Capitol on swearing-in day. (Author's collection)

Jennifer and me campaigning for the US House of Representatives in April 2008. (Author's collection)

Jennifer, the kids, and me on June 19, 2014, after being elected House Majority Whip. (Author's collection)

My chief of staff Brett Horton and me conferring during our walk to the House floor before a vote. (Brendan Smialowski / Getty Images)

Soon after being elected to Congress, I found the congressional baseball game to be a great way to build relationships with my colleagues. One of my favorite memories is when I stole home on Cedric Richmond, pitcher for the Democrats' team. (Photo courtesy of Marty LaVor)

Minutes after this photo of me at second base was taken, nearing the end of our last morning practice, the gunman began his assault on the Republican baseball team. (Photo courtesy of Marty LaVor)

A link in the fence broken by the first bullet fired. From this vantage point, you're looking right at third base, where Congressman Trent Kelly of Mississippi stood. Directly down the baseline is second base, where I was hit a few seconds after the first shot. (Author's collection)

After being shot and unable to run, I dragged myself from second base into the outfield until my arms gave out. My blood left a trail, turning the grass a burnt brown color. (Author's collection)

Thanks to the heroic efforts in the field by Rep. Brad Wenstrup (black ballcap, back to the camera), I made it to the hospital with minutes to spare. Brad is a former combat surgeon who served in Iraq. Also pictured (l to r) are Rep. Mo Brooks, Sen. Jeff Flake, Rep. Gary Palmer, Brian Kelly, Will Batson, and Rep. Steve Pearce. (Photo courtesy of Marty LaVor)

House Chaplain Father Conroy led a bipartisan prayer at second base just before the start of the 2017 Congressional Baseball Game. I was supposed to start at second base. (Win McNamee / Getty Images)

Some of my current and former staff members, along with friends and interns, attended the congressional baseball game on June 15, 2017, one day after the shooting. They knew I would have wanted the game to be played and Team Scalise to be in the stands. (Bill Clark / CQ Roll Call via AP Images)

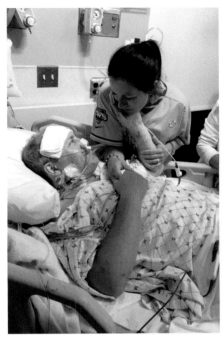

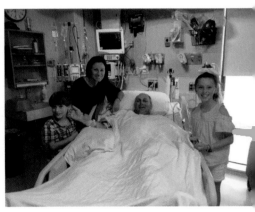

I spent several days after the shooting in shock and sedated for pain management. On Saturday, June 17, 2017, Jennifer and I had our first moments together. Unable to speak because of a breathing tube, I had to communicate with gestures. (Author's collection)

I really wanted to see Madison and Harrison, but those first few days were tough and I was in no condition for them to see me. After several days of waiting, but still in ICU, we were finally reunited. (Author's collection)

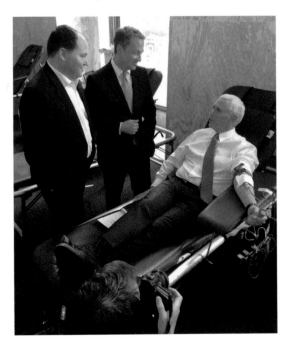

My chief of staff Brett Horton and member services director Bart Reising update Vice President Pence on my condition, while the vice president donates during a blood drive on Capitol Hill on June 20, 2017. (Photo by Sarah Makin-Acciani, Office of the Vice President)

My alma mater, Louisiana State University, named me the honorary coach for the College World Series. The ball used in the first pitch was signed and delivered to me at the hospital. (Author's collection)

"Scalise Strong" shirts could be seen all over the hospital as friends, family, and my medical team gave me daily encouragement. Here, Dr. Jack Sava is pictured with Jennifer, Madison, Harrison, and me. (Author's collection)

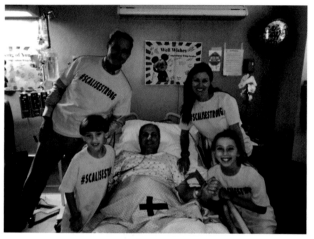

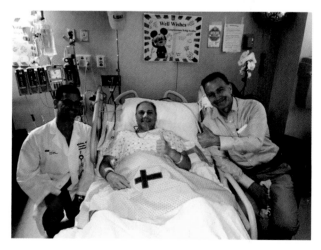

My orthopedic surgeon, Dr. Rob Golden, and my trauma surgeon, Dr. Jack Sava, checking in on me, as they often did during my recovery. Dr. Golden was responsible for piecing me back together and clearing me for rehabilitation. (Author's collection)

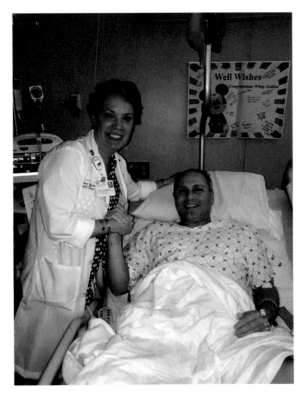

Administrative director of Trauma, Burn, and Critical Care Nurse Susan Kennedy with me. Susan was an integral part of navigating every detail of my recovery and rehabilitation. (Author's collection)

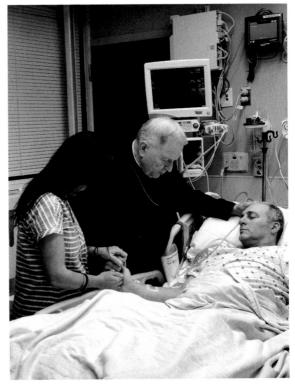

His Excellency Gregory Aymond, Archbishop of New Orleans, prays with Jennifer and me after I was readmitted to ICU in preparation for surgery to address a life-threatening infection. (Author's collection)

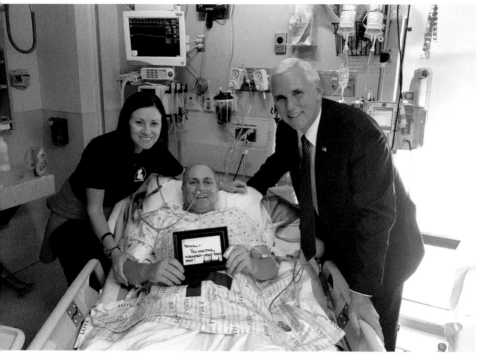

My friend and former House colleague Vice President Mike Pence brings a greeting from President Donald Trump to Jennifer and me while I recover in the ICU. (Author's collection)

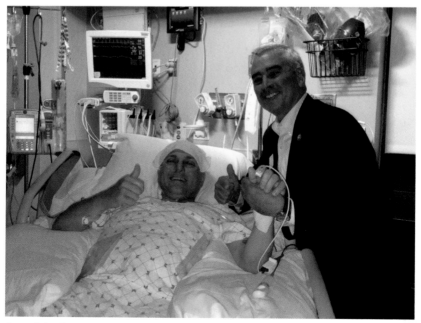

One of the first people to visit me while still in ICU was Brad Wenstrup. Ever the doctor, Brad would come by throughout the summer to check in on me. (Author's collection)

Agents Crystal Griner and David Bailey of the US Capitol Police Dignitary Protection Division— the two agents on duty at the field the day of the shooting—on July 19, 2017. Like me, Crystal had months of rehabilitation and medical procedures ahead of her. (Author's collection)

After more than a month in the hospital, and still weeks from being able to walk even a few steps, I was finally allowed to take a "field trip" outside on July 16, 2017. (Author's collection)

The wheelchair was a welcome upgrade as I was finally cleared for my first physical therapy session at the MedStar gym. (Author's collection)

At MedStar National Rehabilitation Hospital, I spent months learning to walk with the help of physical therapists like Meaghan Minzy and the hospital's Zero-G system. Dr. John Aseff is looking on. (Author's collection)

Jennifer got us these shirts because she saw me as Superman during those months of infections and surgeries, and I saw her as the one person who could handle whatever came her way. (Author's collection)

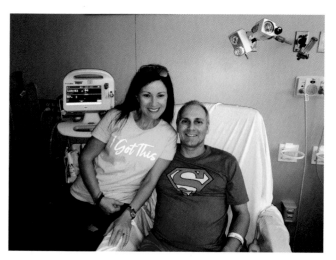

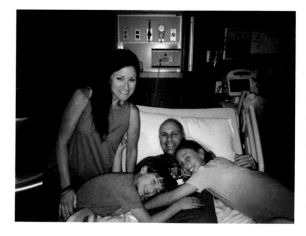

After a long summer for all of us, Harrison and Madison gave me one last hug on August 6, 2017, before leaving Washington, DC, to return to Louisiana so they can begin the new school year. (Author's collection)

Jennifer and me on the Speaker's Porch, minutes before addressing my colleagues in the House Chamber on September 28, 2017. (Author's collection)

LSU's Homecoming Game on September 30, 2017, was really special to me. I was finally back in Louisiana, with life returning to normal. (Author's collection)

During a meeting with congressional leadership about tax reform, President Trump and I visited in the Oval Office, November, 2, 2017. (Official White House Photographer Joyce N. Boghosian)

Jennifer and me at a medal ceremony honoring Special Agents Crystal Griner and David Bailey, November 17, 2018. (Author's collection)

Jennifer and me at the 2017 White House Christmas Party. (Author's collection)

Returning to the Capitol to vote to reopen the government on January 22, 2018, less than an hour after being discharged from yet another surgery days before. (Author's collection)

Serving as captain of the Washington Mardi Gras, January 2018. (Author's collection)

April 17, 2018, right after my final surgery. (Author's collection)

One year to the day after the shooting, I returned to the 2018 Congressional Baseball Game as the starting second baseman, this time proudly wearing my US Capitol Police ballcap. (Author's collection)

Throwing out Rep. Raul Ruiz during the 2018 Congressional Baseball Game. (Cliff Owen / Associated Press)

Celebrating July 4th, 2018. The previous July 4th, I was about to return to the ICU with a near-fatal infection. (Author's collection)

IR was "interventional radiology," another procedure that might help stop the bleeding if this one didn't.

"No," the anesthesiologist said, "I don't like the direction things are going. I think we probably shouldn't leave yet." If a bleeder Sava had closed opened back up in the elevator or the hallway en route to the other room, there'd be no way to stop it. I'd be dead in minutes.

But Sava felt he wasn't making progress fast enough, so he switched tactics. He stopped trying to sew closed the bleeding organs and arteries, and instead, he started pulling out big scissor-like "cross clamps" to squeeze off vessels. The clamps were cumbersome and not a permanent fix because you can't just leave one sticking out of a patient's belly, any more than you could a pair of scissors, but he could move faster with them and stop more bleeding, at least temporarily, in less time.

Soon, it looked like I had a bunch of pairs of scissors jammed into my gut. Sava didn't want to keep them there very long because they weren't closing holes; they were shutting off the blood to whole parts of my body, and they would soon start killing tissue. Since I already had so much dead tissue inside me, whole parts of my body would effectively die, and I'd likely end up with a massive, fatal infection. Sava needed anesthesia to know he wanted to get out of there soon. "What are you guys seeing now?"

The anesthesia team wasn't happy either. No one thought I was improving fast enough.

Sava continued to work. My blood pressure still wasn't improving. Sava asked the people around the table if they thought *now* was a good time to move.

This time, they all agreed, and since he'd let on to what he was thinking when he first started thinking it, they weren't caught off guard; they were ready to mobilize quickly.

The anesthesiologist said, "Yeah, this is about as good as we're going to get," and the plan was in motion.

My abdomen was cut wide open, with foot long retractors pulling the skin apart and exposing my insides to the elements. The risk of infection was high. Beyond that, I had clamps coming out, any one of which could easily jostle free in the chaos of the move, and if that happened, it would start a bleed that would be almost impossible to stop while we were between rooms. But everyone was ready. They were all on the same page. "Okay," Sava said. "We need to get him into IR." Assent came from all around the table, everyone confirming they understood the plan.

"Let's get ready to move."

✛ ✛ ✛

Thus began the second mad dash since arriving at the hospital.

They rolled me out of the OR with my body still cut open, retractors still holding my stomach open as I was raced down the hall. Clamps were sticking out; IVs were everywhere. People holding bags of blood were running alongside; people were pushing wheeled machines now connected to me, including a 300-pound respirator connected to a breathing tube that was lodged in my throat, and the whole menagerie was surrounded by the huge security contingent racing down the hall with us. All these people at full sprint, all swinging around the corner, all pulling into the interventional radiology suite.

Everyone was coordinating. Everyone was on the same page, knowing exactly where we were going and why, so they could keep the clamps from jostling, keep me from losing blood any faster than I already was.

They had to transfer me over to a new table, another delicate operation with my abdomen pulled open and all the tubes and machines and clamps connected to me. Even with all of these pairs of hands working on me, they managed to aviod getting in one another's way, and they got me over to the new bed without me springing any of the dozens of potential leaks.

So far, so good.

They got me onto a table in the middle of a giant, futuristic-looking, half-circle–shaped x-ray machine, and Sava decided it was time to step aside for a moment to try and get someone related to me on the phone. Someone in my family needed to know how serious this was.

As Sava was being patched through to Jennifer, he steeled himself. Notifying next of kin was (and by now, this shouldn't be a surprise) an aspect of the job Sava had read up on— "the science of news delivery." He'd researched how police approached it, and how the military did. He thought for a moment about how he was going to do this. It was tense around him. Tense and crowded. He didn't want to convey any of that to a family member. He didn't want to frighten anyone. He also didn't want to be dishonest. He thought about how he was going to strike that balance, to leave the worst news, if he could, for when my family was there and they could speak in person. He stood in the corner, put the phone to his ear, braced himself for a panicked, hysterical family member, and concentrated so he could get the balance just right.

"Hello?"

A woman's voice came on to the phone, sounding totally calm. It was actually unsettling.

Why is she so casual?

As they began to speak, it seemed to Sava that there was some kind of misconnection. Did he have the wrong number? Was he even speaking to the right person? This woman actually sounded *distracted*, like she was paying more attention to something around her than to what he was telling her. Sava asked, "Do you know when you'll get here?"

"Yeah," Jennifer said. "I'll be up tomorrow for the game."

She'll *what?* "I'm sorry, do you think you can make it sooner?"

"No, I can't make it sooner. The kids have to be at camp." She sounded agitated. He was trying to tell her that her husband was in critical condition, and she actually sounded annoyed that he was disrupting her schedule. "We'll see Steve at the game tomorrow."

Sava was stunned. He could hear a conversation happening in the background; Jen was focusing on something going on in the room at home in Louisiana. Then she came back with a request. "Sorry doctor, could you just put Steve on the line?"

Sava returned to surgery after a surreal conversation, hoping he'd conveyed the severity of the situation, but not at all convinced that he had.

✣ ✣ ✣

As I lay there on the brink of death in the IR suite, Dr. Arshad Khan joined the team and led a procedure, with Dr. Sava helping, that Sava still considers roughly akin to magic. The anesthesia team moved around the room trying to effectively colonize it, turning it into an operating room, stabilizing their machines, getting their equipment positioned just so. Dr. Khan snuck around, under machines and through arms and past the heads of all the people crowded around me, and poked a needle into an artery near my groin.

Through that tiny hole, he carefully fed a wire, with a slight bend in it, farther and farther into my body. Khan could steer the wire by giving it a slight twist, to get the bent end of the wire to face an opening into another arterial branch.

It was like trying to jimmy a car lock by guiding an unfolded hanger past the window seal.

As Khan moved that wire, a little at a time, he watched a monitor. The monitor showed what the x-ray was picking up.

At first, nothing.

Then, with that tiny wire pushed inside my arteries, Dr. Khan squirted a special radiopaque dye that the x-rays don't penetrate. The x-rays bounced off the dye, so on the x-ray machine's monitor, Dr. Khan could see, inside my body, where the dye was going. When he squirted the dye, it looked on the monitor like a lightning bolt had struck—the branching, forking silhouette of my arterial tree, a brief, fleeting picture of my vascular system.

It should have looked like a fine latticework of arteries, a glowing deep-sea coral with thin, fine fingers reaching out.

But it didn't. Now, in the radiology suite, the full scope of the bullet's effect finally came into view: When Khan squirted the dye, he saw not just lightning bolts but, all around the monitor, what looked like fraying cotton balls, like clouds, attached to my arteries. Those clouds were puddles of dye.

That meant the dye wasn't just in my arteries but was also escaping from them.

And that, in turn, meant blood was escaping too.

Each of those clouds represented a tiny wound, where one of the hundreds of pieces of shrapnel had torn through. That solved the mystery—that's why my blood pressure hadn't stabilized, even after Sava had found and clamped so many big bleeds, and even after I'd received so much blood. Those small holes, together, were draining me of blood faster than the anesthesiologists could pump blood in. They'd just been doing it invisibly.

Until now.

With the threat now apparent, the doctors all fell into a rhythm.

✢ ✢ ✢

The different things they were working on all converged to fix this one mechanism composed of so many smaller mechanisms. Sava spoke in his exaggerated, clear way. The anesthesiologists gave me a cocktail of drugs that helped me maintain a livable blood pressure. If they saw it start to fall, they'd twiddle the dials and get it back up to where it'd been a moment ago. At Sava's invitation, they announced how much medication they were giving, when they were giving more, and when they were dialing it back.

Sava, in turn, made a clear, steady announcement that he was removing one of the clamps he'd placed inside me to stop the bleeding. He was going to let me bleed again. The anesthesiologists needed to know, so they wouldn't overreact when they saw a sudden drop in blood pressure and ramp up the drug cocktail too fast.

"I'm coming off with this clamp. You might see a dip."

Then it was Khan's turn. Khan fed that wire past the place Sava had just unclamped, and squirted the dye.

The screen lit up with those forking lightning bolts and the cotton balls sprouting off of them, showing the leaks.

One by one, Khan plugged those tiny holes with a glue-like material, some of them with tiny metal coils. They progressed like that, up my arterial tree, moving bit by bit—Sava removing a clamp, giving the anesthesiologists a heads-up; the anesthesiologists gradually dialing up the drugs as the clamps came off; Khan passing with his wire; all of them coordinating flawlessly, finding their rhythm: clamp, drugs, dye, plug; clamp, drugs, dye, plug; wash, rinse, repeat.

My blood pressure was all over the place, collapsing when Sava let me bleed, ratcheting back up as Khan plugged the dozens of tiny small holes there, collapsing again when Sava removed another clamp. Even as the anesthesiologists, following Sava's calm, measured lead, were careful not to overreact to sudden changes. They had to keep changing the dose of drugs they were giving me to support my blood pressure.

After Sava, Dr. Khan with his magic wire, and the almost supernaturally restrained anesthesia team had been in their rhythm for an hour, removing clamps, finding bleeders, and nailing them, Sava noticed something: The dosages of drugs the anesthesia team was using started to trend down.

It was still back and forth, up and down, but it seemed like the trend line was going down. Like maybe, gradually, anesthe-siology needed less medication to keep me alive.

At the same time, Sava was listening to reports on blood tests. They were constantly taking blood down to the lab, testing it, and then pushing the results to a monitor in the room. Since all the results were "critical values," meaning horrifically abnormal, the lab was also calling a phone in the suite during the operation whenever new results came back, updating the anesthesiologists.

The anesthesiologists, in turn, were repeating some of the values to the room.

Sava was paying attention to how much acid I had in my blood—the more acid in the blood, the less oxygen it was getting. Those numbers were, ever so slightly, beginning to normalize.

Sava felt like he was being shown a thin crack of light. He was seeing hope.

After two hours in the radiology suite, the team felt confi-dent they'd hit all the small holes, all the ones invisible to the naked eye.

Sava still wouldn't allow himself any more optimism beyond telling the team they'd done well and allowing him-self the hope that I still had a chance. He still wasn't confi-dent I'd live. But, for the first time, he felt my chances had improved.

There were still a million things that could go wrong. There were still a million things he could have missed. One of those big bleeders could still pop open, and I'd be dead within a matter of minutes. But he'd made some progress.

✤ ✤ ✤

Sava came out of the IR suite after more than four hours in surgery, but rather than taking a break, he needed to speak again with Jennifer. By that point, he figured she'd be somewhere in the building, or at least close, and it was important she know just how much danger I was in. Sava walked out into a hall full of police, a bunch of members of some kind of commando unit, and Congressman Kevin Brady.

Kevin came up to him. "Hey Doc, how's Steve doing?"

Brett was there too, also trying to find out exactly what was going on with his boss, but Sava was still in a bind. Like Susan Kennedy, he thought he'd seen pretty much everything in his career, but he'd never seen this. He'd been so intensely focused on his patient that it hadn't even occurred to him that there would be public interest in what had happened, and like Susan Kennedy a few hours before, Sava felt he could not answer a very simple question. "How's he doing?"

It wasn't just because he didn't know if I'd ever wake up again. Even saying "Fine" or "Not great" felt to him like it'd be disclosing my personal medical information. He didn't have my consent to do that. Was there a different protocol when the patient was an elected official? Did elected officials somehow forfeit the same rights to privacy? Was there some principle of "the public has a right to know"?

Sava didn't know, but didn't think so. He was encountering perhaps the single eventuality he had not taken it upon himself to study and ponder in his personal time.

Besides, whatever the law was, he had no doubt about the ethics: He was committed to the patient he was trying to save. He felt totally obligated to me, a person he didn't know, had never spoken to, and maybe *would* never speak to. He wasn't committed to my friends, or even to the public, and wouldn't say anything to them unless explicitly permitted by next of kin. As soon as he saw Jennifer, they'd clear all that up. He could stonewall people for a few more minutes. He tried to politely dodge Kevin.

Then Brett came up to Sava and broke the news—Jen wasn't there, and in fact, she was not even close.

Jen had not even left Louisiana.

Brett saw something turn in Sava. No more messing around. No more "science of news delivery." Sava was going to tell Jen whatever he needed to tell her to jolt her out of it, get her in the air, and get her to the hospital, so that she would get to see me before I died, which could happen at any moment.

And while he was at it, he was going to get her to tell him who else he could speak to, so the hospital could begin correcting all the false information circulating.

On the phone, Jen said she was finally en route and gave Sava permission to read Brett in to what was going on. When he did, explaining to Brett just how close to death I was, Brett went ghost white. He'd had no idea. He hadn't been prepared.

Brett was now the only visitor who knew the gravity of my condition. All around him, my friends and colleagues gathered, behaving like you'd behave if your friend had a minor leg injury and you were killing time before going in to write something funny on his cast and cheer him up.

Brett now knew that was not the situation at all. He had to leave everyone and find a place in the hospital where he could sit by himself, away from everyone, because their mood was so dissonant with what he'd just learned.

Afternoon

When Jen first arrived, after dropping the kids off at the hotel, Dr. Sava figured she'd still be in shock. Based on their strange phone conversations earlier in the day and the fact that she'd been more agitated about the change to the kids' schedule than her husband's condition, Sava figured she still wasn't processing the situation.

Within an hour, that perception totally changed.

The two of them would become like co-captains of a ship coming to rescue me. The truth is Jen was still, somehow, protected from truly internalizing just how close to death I was, but it was no longer denial. She was in a hospital surrounded by the people trying to help me, and when she came into the room, she didn't see her jovial, laughing husband, but a body lying inert, woven through with tubes and wires, looking more dead than alive.

Now, it was more a conscious decision to maintain poise. She knew panic wouldn't do me any good. By that point, the children were safe in the hotel, they'd survived the trip to D.C., they'd survived the airports, so Jen was no longer worried about a second assassin coming after the family. With the children safe, she could focus on me.

So that afternoon, Jen began to show gratitude to all of the hospital staff, even amid the chaos and strain. She was proactively warm, so people *wanted* to speak to her, rather than to pull away, as is sometimes natural when dealing with the wife of the guy with the iffy prognosis and all the security officers. She put people at ease. She disarmed them. She made sure they all knew she didn't expect any kind of special treatment, and she made clear that she wouldn't—at least, at that point—be second-guessing their decisions.

Dr. Sava began to observe Jen closely, because he could tell her way of handling the crisis was going to be useful. She had a bit of what Sava had seen in that doctor back when Sava was a student: a way of getting teams to perform better. He actually thought he could learn from her. He recognized in her a sense of empathy that seemed to be a big part of the connection she was forming so quickly with the doctors and nurses. She showed impulse control, too. He assumed she was probably, on some level, terrified, and he knew from their phone calls that at least earlier in the day, she'd been annoyed with the people telling her what to do, including him. Yet once she got to the hospital, she showed no sense of impatience with the staff, no indication that, whether because of exhaustion or emotion or both, she might lash out. She made it abundantly clear that no one needed to walk on eggshells around her. Every single person involved in trying to save me heard from Jen some version of "You're the expert. We appreciate what you're doing. We trust you." She made it abundantly clear that she was not going to add to the pressure they were already under.

In fact, she was going to take some pressure off.

The situation was already bigger and more complicated than any they'd dealt with before. All the extraneous demands on their time—dealing with the press and the public; hallways crowded with not just friends but security, members of Congress and staff—put extra strain on the medical team and threatened to get in the way of my treatment. Immediately upon arriving, Jen could see what was happening. So, she came in and tried to pull all those nonmedical tasks off Sava's plate and onto her own. She would take on the task of dealing with the press, communicating with colleagues, and dealing with my whip office, all the things that would otherwise have kept the care team from focusing only on the patients.

Sava was astounded. Jen was somehow at once both deferential and in control; at once both deeply appreciative and entirely self-sufficient. In this woman who'd just walked into the hospital, he'd been given a human textbook for how to support the care team trying to save a loved one. Sava didn't care that Jen had no medical training. He came to trust her opinion and, at critical times, would solicit it. To Jen, Sava was the man trying to save her husband's life, and to Sava, Jen was the person giving him the best chance of doing so.

✧ ✧ ✧

They also had something else in common—they both had surreal interactions with the White House that day. Jennifer had already spoken to President Trump once, before she took off from New Orleans that afternoon, and the president had tried to check in with the hospital, too. Earlier in the day, Sava couldn't disclose information to anyone; he couldn't even accommodate the president 's desire for information about my status.

But by that night, Sava had consent from Jen to begin briefing people, and the first time he was asked about my recovery, he said, "Recovery? I'm not thinking about recovery. I'm thinking about getting him through the night."

After an unsettling update, the president wanted to see Jen. Brett came into the hospital room to tell Jen the president of the United States was waiting to see her.

But Jen, along with Rick, Karen, and Father Tim, the priest from the kids' Catholic school who happened to be in D.C. for the summer, had only recently been allowed into the room to see me, and Jen wasn't leaving my side.

"He's welcome to come in. I'm sure it would mean a lot to Steve," Jen said. So a few minutes later, after some more back and forth, agents with earpieces filed into the ICU, followed by the president and first lady, everyone crowding into that one small room.

As soon as he got in the room, the president gave Jen a bear hug. The first lady came over and gave Jen another big hug, whispered a few encouraging words, and handed her a giant bouquet of flowers.

"Well," the president said, going over to our friends, "who do we have here?" He introduced himself to Karen, Rick, and Father Tim, asking all their names, shaking their hands; all of them were impressed by how friendly he was in person. Jen thought he seemed genuinely concerned, but a little uncomfortable; he seemed to be trying to avoid looking at me. Like maybe he thought it'd be rude to do so.

"Mr. President," Jen said, "why don't you tell Steve 'Hello'? I really think he can hear us. I think he'd be honored."

And the president did. At Jen's urging, he came to the head of the bed and leaned toward me. He turned back to Jen. "He looks good!"

Jen thought, *No he doesn't!* But she was touched by the gesture, and she was moved, when she stopped to consider it, just by the fact that the leader of the free world had taken time, on his birthday no less, to spend a few moments with her. It provided a much-needed distraction, a much-needed morale boost, just as Jen was beginning to face what would turn out to be the most difficult time of her life.

✢ ✢ ✢

That evening, Sava found himself in his office with Jen, Brett, my other chief of staff Megan Bel Miller (who runs my personal office, which is focused on my Louisiana constituents, while Brett runs my whip office), the hospital's press team, Kevin Brady, chief deputy whip Patrick McHenry, Majority Leader Kevin McCarthy, and Susan Kennedy, all of them meeting about a one-paragraph statement to the press. It was like a committee meeting, held in Sava's office, and chaired by Jen, just because everyone kept deferring to her, and she clearly had the best ideas about how to handle all the added attention.

Sava was relegated—happily, but surreally—to taking dictation. A head trauma surgeon, the guy who, in just about every TV show, is the cocky, chauvinistic fighter ace, was playing the role of secretary, as the team turned over each word. "How will the public interpret 'critical'? Will they know what it means?"

When they were finished, and they'd all agreed on the wording, Sava checked it one last time and sent it off to the hospital media relations department.

And then, finally, after a long, crazy, nonstop day, he left for the night.

As he pulled up to his house, he had a moment of total confusion.

There, on the big-screen TV he could see through the living room window, was the document they'd all just been working on in his office.

Are my monitors somehow screen sharing?

It wasn't until the screen changed to an anchor behind the news desk that he realized what was going on—the evening news was showing the document he'd typed up in his office minutes ago.

This was to be Sava's new normal.

Thursday

Through Wednesday night, I was unconscious. Oblivious to everything going on above me, everything around me. Still back and forth from the brink.

Jen was at the hospital all day and well into the night, leaving only because the kids wouldn't go to sleep without her, and it was already getting close to midnight.

This would become her pattern: At the hospital all day, trying to show only positivity when she was around me (because she swore that, even unconscious, I could hear her); trying to show only positivity for the doctors; then going back to the hotel and trying to show only positivity to the kids.

Only after the kids were asleep did she feel she could let her guard down, just a little, sitting out on the hotel room's balcony with a friend or relative, talking, opening up a bit, crying, worrying, decompressing, until she'd let off enough pressure that she could finally sleep at 3:00 AM, 4:00 AM, at 7:00 AM, if she slept at all.

I'd been touch and go. I'd undergone another surgery in which the orthopedic surgeon, Dr. Robert Golden, started the process of repairing my shattered pelvis and femur. He had to drill a hole, roll a rod into it, and rebuild a bow and socket, shoring up the hip and pelvis with metal, so that if I ever woke up, I'd have some hope of eventually, one day, learning to walk again.

I hadn't been conscious since I went into shock en route to the hospital the day before. Jen fervently believed, even without any evidence, that eventually I'd wake up, but she had no idea when, and she knew she wouldn't be able to keep the shooting from the kids forever—mostly because they were really excited for the baseball game.

But they're also very sensitive, intuitive kids, and they knew, on some level, that something was wrong. Mom had it under control, because mom always has everything under control, but something wasn't right. They trusted she wouldn't let them down, and they were trying, in their own way, to give her a pass. Trying not to push mom too much, to not question or challenge her too forcefully; trying to give her a bit of a break.

But just a bit of one.

Soon, they'd start to worry.

When the kids woke up the morning after "Donald Trump's birthday party"—meaning Jen's trip to the hospital, where I lay unconscious, woven through with wires, a machine breathing for me, and tubes coming out of my throat, my nose, my stomach, and both sides of my neck—they wanted to know where I was. They were full of energy. Jen hadn't slept even an hour.

"Where's Daddy?"

"Oh, darn! He just left before y'all woke up. Y'all just missed him! He had to leave early for baseball practice. Tonight's the big game."

"Oh, man! Can we go watch him practice?"

"Well, by now, he's probably already done. He's at work now."

"Can we go visit Daddy at work?"

"No, you have to wait."

Jen was working on two days with almost no sleep, and she was needed back at the hospital.

"I have a meeting though. At...I have a meeting at Daddy's office."

Jen never meets me at the office.

"I have to go to Daddy's office. I have to go help Daddy with some things there. It's nothing fun for y'all. Miss Ellen and Miss Stephanie are gonna stay, and y'all are going to play games."

Another dodge.

She wasn't going to be able to maintain it much longer. The Congressional Baseball Game was now in a matter of hours. The kids knew that; they had their tee-shirts emblazoned with "Team Scalise" ready to go. They love the game as much as I do. It's one of their favorite rites of summer, and the only way Jen could avoid telling them what had happened any longer would be to pretend she forgot about them. To just not come back from the hospital, abandon her own kids, tell them they'd slipped her mind. She'd never do that.

On the other hand, if they knew that all these sudden schedule changes they were still in the middle of—the sudden trip, skipping summer camp, staying in a hotel—were because someone had tried to kill their father and he might never wake up.... Well, she couldn't do that to them either. She couldn't worry them with such a disturbing situation, while their lives were still being dictated by it.

She was stuck. She had only bad options. And with the game just a few hours away, she was running out of time.

✣ ✣ ✣

Meanwhile, my friends started coming in from all over the country to do what they could. To be there for Jen, to be there for me. My sister Tara flew up from Tampa, even though she was in the middle of her own fight. Tara was battling breast cancer, the same evil disease that took our mother, Carol, from us 18 years earlier. Mom was only 59. She'd seemed almost immortal to me, and to Tara as well, I think. Even after she was diagnosed, it seemed for years like Mom was too much for cancer. She beat it, and it came back, but she still went to work every day, even in the middle of chemo. Since she passed, I'd always felt like she was my guardian angel. I'm certain she was out there over that ball field with me that day, helping God coordinate all the little miracles that saved us, and giving me a fighting chance to survive.

When Tara heard what had happened, she insisted on coming to be near me. Her doctors told her she couldn't go, that her immune system was too weakened by chemo for a plane ride. She made it clear she was not asking them for permission. She was *going* to travel. She was just asking their advice on the safest way to get to me. They eventually relented, giving her a yellow (not green) light, and she left to check on her buddy.

I'd shown no sign of waking up. The media was in a frenzy. Chris Bond and Lauren Fine, who made up my press team, were inundated with requests, but Sava still wasn't comfortable updating the information they'd released the night before: I remained in critical condition. Saying anything more optimistic than that would be inaccurate. That was it.

That night, as I lay in a coma, my colleagues gathered over at the baseball stadium. They'd decided that playing the game was what I would have wanted (and they were right). Before the game, all the players, Republicans and Democrats, came together and gathered around second base, where I would have started, and together, they prayed for me. Up in the broadcast booth, Republican speaker Paul Ryan and Democratic leader Nancy Pelosi came together in front of TV cameras for their first ever joint interview. The game would raise more money than any of the games before it—a million and a half dollars for three local children's charities and the Capitol Police Memorial Fund, thanks to the 25,000-person-strong crowd, two and a half times the usual attendance. It was a bigger crowd, coming out to see a bunch of middle-aged guys bumble across the field, than attend some Major League games.

None of that was much comfort to Jen.

As the game got under way, she was in a car on the way back to the hotel, struggling with how she was going to tell the children what was really going on. Struggling, really, with how she was going to protect them. And for the first time, she broke down.

Until then, no one had seen even the slightest hint of the burden she was carrying. She was at the hospital all night, as I lay there, in my oblivion, unable to provide her any comfort, buried in tubes and wires and beeping monitors. After spending countless hours at the hospital, she'd returned to the hotel—her only moment of calm was seeing the sun rising over the Capitol dome. Then she went to sleep and woke up 45 minutes later when the kids woke up.

Then, back to the hospital.

She'd finally reached a point where there was no way to avoid talking with the kids, because the kids knew the game was happening and, if I wasn't there, they'd know something must be very wrong. Now she had to tell them. She had no idea how she was going to do that. She wept during the car ride back to the hotel for the first time, showing just a bit of the pressure she'd been under.

She arrived at the hotel, went up in the elevator, and tried to compose herself as she walked slowly down the hall.

As she neared their room, though, she began to hear their voices from behind their door. They were laughing and shrieking in excitement; it was time to go see Daddy at the game!

Jen could feel herself about to break down. She couldn't face them. She couldn't let them see her like that. She veered off into Rick and Karen's room, and there, she wept again, overwhelmed by the weight that had fallen on her.

But only for a moment. She gave herself a minute to let the pressure get to her, then she snapped her fingers, tried to compose herself, and tried to summon confidence. A calmness came over her. She felt a burden being lifted from her. She had a window in which to do what needed to be done, but she didn't know how long it was going to stay open, how long she could keep the feelings at bay, and if the kids saw her lose her composure, they'd know things were very bad. They needed at least one parent right now. Jen patted her eyes, painted a smile on her face, and headed for the door.

Karen saw her get up to leave. "What are you going to say?"

"I don't know. I don't know. I'll figure it out. I've just gotta

get it over with. Let's go. I gotta go." She hurried to the kids'
room next door, trying to get there before she lost her nerve.
Rick and Karen followed a few paces behind. Jen motored into
the children's room, moving quickly, feeling the need to do
this *now*. Before she broke down.

Ellen and Stephanie were in the room keeping an eye on
the kids, but when they saw Jen hustle in, they knew what was
about to happen and made a beeline out of the room to give
Jen some privacy.

Jen forced herself to smile. She looked at the kids' smiling
faces and saw that they were wearing their shirts with my face
on them. They were ready for the game. When they saw Jen,
they cheered.

"Let's go, we're late!"

"Okay, wait." Jen took a breath. "I have to talk to you guys
about something."

Maddie already looked worried. Just like that, in just a
split second, like she'd sensed all along something was wrong
and knew this moment was coming.

"What's wrong?" Maddie asked. "Mommy, what's wrong?"
And even before Jen could say anything else, Maddie asked,
"What's wrong with Daddy?"

"Nothing. Nothing! Just listen."

She still didn't know what she was going to say.

"Just sit on the bed. Everything's fine!"

"Where's Daddy?"

"Daddy's *fine*. Don't start panicking. Just sit and let me tell
you what happened today. It's a crazy story!"

By then, Jen knew she had to tell them some version of
what had happened, but she also knew she didn't want the kids

to have an image in their heads of someone pointing a gun at their dad. Not yet, not while they were so young, not while my future was still uncertain.

Jen just started talking, like she had started talking the morning before in New Orleans when the kids woke up, just repeating whatever came to her mind, as if someone else was whispering into an earpiece and her job was just to recite what she was told.

"You know how we always talk about how sometimes people do really crazy things and they make really bad decisions? We always talk about making good choices and bad choices."

She forced her voice to sound casual.

"At Daddy's baseball practice, someone was there, and he made a really bad choice."

"Who?"

"Well, I don't really know the person, but he made a really bad choice. He thought it was a good idea to come to practice and watch, and he brought a gun with him. He thought it was a good idea to shoot the gun up in the air! And he thought it was funny. Bullets came falling down, and one of them hit your Daddy in the hip. It really wasn't a good choice."

Maddie screamed. She started gasping, nearly hyperventilating, and then Harrison did too.

Now Jen had two panicking kids in front of her, and she was trying as hard as she could not to join them. Even though seeing her two babies so upset broke her heart, she had to make it seem like they were being completely unreasonable. She tried to make herself sound amused by their disproportionate reaction. She forced herself to smile again and tried to make herself laugh.

"Baby! Why are you so upset? Don't be so upset! I'm not even finished telling you the story. Don't be upset already!"

Maddie was screaming. "I want to go right now! Where is he?"

"Oh, he's at the hospital."

"I want to go right now!"

Jen didn't want the kids to see me hovering on the brink of death. Just like the image of someone trying to hurt their father, she didn't want the image of their father fighting for his life, with tubes in his throat, his nose, coming out both sides of his neck, to be in their minds for the rest of their lives.

"Whoa, whoa. Wait. Just wait a minute. We can't go to the hospital just yet. His doctor is taking really good care of him, and he's resting right now while he recovers from surgery."

"SURGERY?!"

It was like a whole new punch in the gut.

"Surgery for what?!"

"No, no. They just had.... The bullet went right there under the skin. It broke a couple of his bones."

"Is he going to be okay?"

"Yes."

Maddie looked at Jen and said, in a stern, aggressive voice, "How do you *KNOW* he's going to be okay?!"

"Because doctors are taking good care of him, and I trust them. And God is in control."

That seemed to calm Maddie, for the time being. She took a breath. But she was still struggling to process this. Even with Jen's inspired effort, it was like she'd just walked into the room and blurted out, "Someone wanted to kill your dad, and so now your dad's probably dead." Jen tried as hard as she could to keep it together. She fought back tears. She fought to make it look like she wasn't trying to fight back tears. She pushed on.

"It just broke a couple of bones! They just had to go in and take the bullet out and fix some of his bones. It's just like when your friends break their arms or their legs and you see their casts on them! It's just like that. It's just like breaking your leg or your arm falling off a trampoline. That's all it is! It's not a big deal, okay? But he's sleepy. They had him on some medicine to make him feel better, and it has him sleeping. We can't really go there right now. Right now, where he's located, just because he's out of surgery, kids can't go there."

For a moment, it was calm. The kids were in tears, but they'd quieted down now, struggling to process.

Jen noticed that our son, who's the kindest, most low-key, adaptable boy in the world, had an angry look on his face. He was actually gritting his teeth. This was new. They were all in unchartered territory now. Jen wanted him to be able to come out with whatever was on his mind. "So, do either of you have any questions?"

Harrison did. "What happened to the guy who was shooting?"

"Well—" It hadn't occurred to her she might need to answer that question. "Well, you know how we always talk about what Daddy's detail does, and why they're with Daddy? Y'all always worry about it, and y'all don't want Daddy to have to need them. But thank goodness Daddy had them, because they were there with him. They were able to stop this crazy person from putting out any more bullets."

That wasn't quite good enough.

"*Who* stopped him?"

"Mr. Dave and Ms. Crystal."

"*Good.* Did they kill him?"

Jen was taken aback. How did this kind of question even occur to our kind-hearted son? She was exhausted, though, and she'd just about tapped out her well of creativity. However ugly what she told them might be, she figured if she ignored the question, their own imaginations would fill the gaps and make it worse. She decided just to relent.

"Yeah. They did."

Still not good enough for Harrison. "*Who* killed him?"

"Mr. Dave."

And for some reason, that gave my son the release he needed. Jen could see it on his face. His expression softened, the muscles in his face relaxed, and though he was still crying, he pumped his fist and said, "*Yes!*"

Jen was shocked. "Baby, do you really understand what that means?"

"It means he can't hurt Daddy anymore."

✣ ✣ ✣

By Friday, Sava was finally willing to say, publicly, that I was showing some signs of improvement. I was still in critical condition. I was still in a coma. But my vital signs had been creeping in the right direction.

There was still no guarantee that I'd wake up. And if I did wake up, there was no telling whether I was going to be the same person. On the day of the shooting, my brain had been deprived of oxygen for crucial minutes before I got to the operating room, before the Massive Transfusion Protocol began. So Jen had to try to prepare herself for what I'd be like with brain damage. If I woke up, would I be a vegetable? Would I be dependent and nonresponsive for the rest of my life?

Meanwhile, Brett's schedule was better than Jen's, but just barely. He was keeping vigil too. Brett, along with Charles and Megan, served as a greeter for all the people stopping by to check in. They coordinated all the good wishes and prayers happening around me, my friends coming to be with Jen for a bit, Cedric coming again, my sister defying her own doctors to be near me, my friends flying up from home. All these people converged on the hospital. They were there for Jen and there for me, and I had no idea. Conversations happened over me, about me; people speaking in hushed tones as if it mattered, as if I was just dozing off and might wake up.

Friday

Day Three.

On Friday, Speaker of the House Paul Ryan and his wife, Janna, came by.

Jen took them into the ICU room. Paul and Janna sat to one side of the bed, Jen on the other, and they began to chat.

As I lay there unconscious, Paul and Jen each holding one of my hands, Janna sitting a little behind, Paul began asking questions. Just general questions. "How's he doing?" "Have things improved?" Nothing specific, nothing too pointed. But as Paul spoke, his voice filling the room, Jen noticed something.

Are Steve's eyes fluttering?

She saw it again. She wasn't just imaging things. "Paul, he's trying to open his eyes. Did you see that? He's trying to open his eyes!"

Paul began to choke up. "Really?"

Jen egged him on. "Keep talking! He hears your voice! Keep talking, and let's try to get him to do it again!"

"Um…uh…." Paul, now on the spot, was trying to think of what to say. Jen had an idea.

"Tell him about the red snapper bill! Steve doesn't know what happened!"

The shooting had happened just before we were set to announce the new red snapper compromise, so at Jen's urging, Paul launched into an extensive briefing about exactly what had happened with the red snapper announcement—the ins and outs and specific policy terms, how it was received, politics and policy—and as he went through his impromptu briefing on the finer points of sport-fishing policy, Jen felt her hand being squeezed.

Paul looked up. He'd felt it too.

Jen nearly screamed. Paul's face lit up. My hands had, ever so slightly, squeezed theirs.

And then, Jen swore, my eyes opened.

Just a sliver, not even a third of the way, and just for a second or two, then they closed.

It didn't quite look like I was waking up. She saw no recognition in my eyes. They had a glassy, vacant look, like I was having a seizure maybe, but she knew it wasn't a seizure. It was hope. Jen knew she wasn't crazy because Paul had seen it too, the first sign of life I'd shown since I'd lost consciousness.

But if it seemed like a sign that the worst was behind us, it was a misleading one, because I was not, in fact, waking up.

I was taking a turn for the worse.

✛ ✛ ✛

As I lay there oblivious to what was going on around me, my body threw more riddles at those looking after me, this time at Sava and his team.

That afternoon, around the time Paul and Janna left, my lactic acid levels started to rise.

That told Sava something was very wrong, but not *what*. It indicated cells were being starved of oxygen, but that could be due to any number of catastrophic problems.

It was like the blinking "RED ALERT" warning light on the Starship *Enterprise*. You know you might be about to crash, but you don't know why. It could have been that I was going back into shock. It could have been that I was bleeding out from somewhere. It could have been that there was a bad infection my medical team had missed or that my heart was failing.

Worse yet, you don't get those numbers immediately, so whatever the problem was, it had started hours before they even noticed it.

The team scrambled. They ran tests; they examined me up and down; then they ran more tests. They couldn't find any of the things they thought could be wrong.

The levels kept rising as Sava and his team tried to solve the puzzle before it was too late.

Eventually, curiously, the numbers normalized. For no apparent reason. It was a welcome development, but a mysterious one. *Something* had caused the system to start blinking red. It was only much later, after several more lactic acid scares, that Sava and his team established I just naturally had abnormally twitchy acid levels. They could spike for any number of reasons, without necessarily indicating any of the catastrophic system failures those numbers usually do.

Now reasonably comfortable that the scare was over, and that he could take a deep breath, Sava went to a banquet to fulfill another one of his roles: delivering a roast of the chief residents who were about to become surgeons, and introducing awards.

As he spoke before a podium, his phone buzzed with a text message. He held his phone below the podium so the crowd couldn't see, and he read it as he spoke. The message was from his partner, Dr. Shiflett.

CK is way up.

Another very bad sign. CK meant creatine kinase. It's an enzyme that, if it was indeed up, meant that inside me, tissue had started dying. The text went on:

I think he's got a compartment syndrome.
We may need to take him back emergently.

Compartment syndrome is when part of the body is under such fierce swelling that it starts to squeeze off its own blood supply. Without blood, tissue death accelerates until that entire part of the body is effectively dead and requires amputation. It causes kidney failure, infection—a whole cascade of life-threatening complications.

Sava snuck away from the podium for a moment and asked Shiflett by phone to hold off. As soon as he could, Sava bolted from the banquet back to the hospital to try to figure out what was going on. His fear was exacerbated by the fact that, like the scare they'd just had, this number too came with a delay. It didn't tell him something bad was starting; it told him something bad had been going on for hours.

He got back to the hospital and examined me closely, looking for signs of worse than usual swelling so he could help decide if I was going to need emergency surgery. After a frantic several hours, he finally found the cause for the alarm: The levels were indicating tissue death after all, just not compartment syndrome. The levels had spiked because so much tissue had died inside me as a result of the bullet fragments tearing through my body. Tissue was continuing to die, and the CK levels were spiking, even days after the shooting.

The CK levels eventually settled too. Even though those two scares turned out to be false alarms, they both happened late into the night, so Sava was soon on Jen and Brett's sleep schedule, which is to say, he basically wasn't sleeping at all.

Until finally, after two apparent disasters were seemingly averted, he went home to spend a couple of hours with his family and fell asleep, with his daughter's head on his chest.

✠ ✠ ✠

The next major predicament was breathing.

I couldn't breathe on my own. I wasn't strong enough. And I needed more oxygen than normal because the trauma had caused so much acid in my blood, and oxygen is how you burn it off.

They had to breathe for me, so they had put a breathing tube down my throat and hooked it up to a respirator. Even though I'd lost consciousness, they now had me on a heavy dose of propofol to make sure I didn't wake up. They didn't want me to be awake with that breathing tube in, or at least not for very long, because it's frightening and painful to be awake with a plastic tube jammed down your throat.

The problem was that although I needed the breathing tube to survive, it was also dangerous to have it in. It put me at greater risk for infection and other complications, like pneumonia, because that plastic tube is effectively a highway past all my natural defenses against foreign invaders. I couldn't cough to expel dust or dirt; the tube went right past the little cilia in my lungs that help keep things out. Plus, as long as they kept the breathing tube in, they needed to keep me unconscious. The longer I was unconscious, though, the greater the risk of blood clots, pressure sores, and other complications that happen when you're not moving at all and not breathing on your own.

Conversely, the drug they used to keep me unconscious, propofol, also depresses breathing. If they were going to take the tube out, they certainly couldn't keep giving me a drug that slowed breathing.

So every day, Sava and the team met to discuss whether they could get away with taking the breathing tube out or whether they had no choice but to keep me sedated.

There'd been the acid level scare, then the compartment syndrome scare, but on Friday night, into Saturday morning, things had evened out for a bit. Just long enough that the doctors thought they could get away with doing little tests, like dialing down the percentage of oxygen on the breathing machine and seeing how my body handled it. At that point, I didn't have another surgery scheduled in the immediate future—surgery would have required a breathing tube—so Sava and the team decided it was time to cut the propofol, see if I woke up, and see if they could get away with removing the breathing tube.

They planned to wait until they had a full complement of staff at the hospital, in case something went wrong. They'd have to let me wake up with the breathing tube still in, for awhile at least, because if I *couldn't* handle breathing on my own, they needed to be able to get me air quickly. So the plan was to let me wake up, see how I did breathing, and if I did okay, let me stay awake and take the tube out. They didn't want to keep the tube in any longer—or risk infection any more—than they absolutely had to.

It was time to find out whether they absolutely had to.

Sava's team kept the pain medications flowing but abruptly shut off the flow of propofol.

Then they waited and watched.

Saturday

A few minutes after taking ground balls at second base, I'm awake. I'm inside some kind of a fog.

I'm in a room.

Plain room. Plain curtains.

Bland.

Colorless.

A hospital; that much is clear.

Very little is clear other than that.

There's Brett. *Hi, Brett.*

Is my wife here?

I'm thirsty. I have some Gatorade over in the dugout. Can someone get me that—only I'm not on the field anymore. I need Jen. Why isn't Jennifer here? For some reason, it feels like Jen should be nearby, even though I came off the field a few minutes ago, with Jen a thousand miles away in New Orleans.

I'm getting confused by time. I'm trying to hold onto a few different timelines, and that sense of comprehension is just out of reach. It's like there's a big damp cloud encasing my brain. I can't access my senses; they're foggy and refracted. The part of my mind that converts sights and sounds into *understanding things* is dead. Everything is dead, or asleep. My body is dead or asleep. It has been jangled into paralysis by bullet fragments zipping around and shocking things to sleep, by pieces of metal passing through my trunk at 2,000 meters per second, shattering pelvis, femur, hip, puncturing organs and juddering nerves.

My eyes are open.

Man, am I thirsty. What day is it? Jen would know. Is Jen here?

"Is Jen here?" When I try to ask the question, nothing happens. The apparatus I'm trying to activate in order to make sound is jammed. Or it's dead. My throat feels like a piece of stiff plastic. It's like a microphone that won't turn on. It's like it doesn't belong to me anymore.

My voice is gone.

"You have a breathing tube in," someone says, someone up above who knows I'm struggling, or who can read minds.

Someone puts a pen in my hand and holds a piece of paper for me so I can write words. But I can barely move my arm. It's extremely heavy and hard to control. It feels like my arm itself is sedated; trying to move it is like moving through high water in a dream. I try to make a "J" for "Jen" but I know it can't possibly look like a J. I don't know how to do this. I don't know how I'm going to make an "e." I feel almost like she's near me, and if I could just figure out a way to make an "e".... I put the tip of the pen to the paper again, wondering how I'm going to get my hand to work, how I'm ever going to communicate, with anyone, ever again, and if I can't communicate, how I'm going to figure out where I am and what's happening and where my wife—

"Wait," Brett speaks up. "Jennifer? Are you trying to say Jennifer?"

A flood of relief. I nod yes.

"She's on her way. We woke her up; she's on her way."

For a moment, that calms me.

✤ ✤ ✤

It's later now. Jen is here and finding a way through the tubes and lines, like a diamond thief contorting herself around a laser grid alarm system, to hug me. I don't know it's been four whole days since I was last awake, so I don't know why seeing her is so overpowering, why I'm suddenly given strength in my arms, but once I have her in my grasp, I'm crying, and I can't let her go. I have to hold her so tightly, and for so long, that my fingers leave marks on her skin.

Then I'm agitated again.

There's something I need to know. Something I'm trying to recall.

I'm thinking of the one clear sense I remember. I'm holding in my mind the sound I heard just a few minutes ago on the baseball field, the sound of different kinds of weapons firing. The sound of a *shootout*.

I'm sedated; there are opiates coursing through my system, slowing everything down, but through the fog, I finally grasp and hold that thought long enough to ask the question, before it has a chance to squirm away from me again: Someone in my security detail is hurt. I look at Jen. I *will* my arms, which have gone weak again, to come up to my chest. I *will* my fingers into the shape of a pistol.

It takes her a minute. Then a look of understanding comes over her face.

"You're in the hospital; you were shot."

No! In my mind, I yell. *I know that! That's not what I mean!* This is a minor form of torture—needing to know things without being able to ask them. Like having the world's worst itch and my arms in a straightjacket.

I try again, miming a pistol.

She asks, "Are you trying to ask about the shooter?"

I shake my head. *No!* I'm not asking about the shooter! I'm frustrated.

"Detail? Are you asking about Dave and Crystal?"

Yes! Yes! I nod to signal *yes.*

"Dave and Crystal are fine. Crystal was hit, but she's okay."

Some coiled part of me releases, relaxes just a bit. I feel tears come to my eyes again.

"She's in the hospital. She's going to be fine. Dave's doing great. They're both here; they're both asking about you."

Another moment of relief. One less concern, one less question to communicate.

This is how it would be for the next month. Fogginess leading to confusion, confusion leading to frustration, and then occasionally, the simple, sweet relief of being able to locate a question floating around in my mind, grab it, ask it, and have it answered. The relief of knowing something I'd wanted to know, if only for a moment, before forgetting again. Calmness comes with every new sense of comprehension. So I'd have to learn to take calmness in small doses.

I ramp up for another question. It takes effort. There's something else I need to know. Something based on what Jen said. I don't know what other hand signals I can make. So I just try the same one again. I put my hands together. Again, I point my fingers forward, the same hand pistol gesture I'd used before.

This time, somehow, Jen understands right away.

"The shooter," she says. "They got him."

✤ ✤ ✤

Amid the confusion and the separate timelines I was trying to keep straight, this felt like justice prevailing. I felt it
as another powerful sense of relief. *They got him.* It's strange
to be calmed by a man's death. It's upsetting, in the same way
it's upsetting to hear your son celebrating someone dying,
but I think it came from the same place. When I heard what
Harrison said—"He can't hurt Daddy anymore"—I thought
there was truth to that. My son was thinking *physically;* he
was relieved by the idea that someone who'd hurt me couldn't
hurt anyone else. For me, in my muddled state, the gunman
represented something troubling and confusing, and knowing
he was dead erased a vague sense of some evil still lurking out
there, hurting other people, or even of some kind of sensation-
alized trial with this man's face on the news, a prolonged saga.
There was a very simple feeling of goodness prevailing, like a
satisfying wrap-up to a movie, the kind you don't usually get
in real life. Everything is okay. The good guys won. The bad
guy lost. The world righted itself.

For a moment, things were settled.

Although, like in the movies, the relief was momentary. In
truth, it wasn't quite so simple.

✤ ✤ ✤

When the CIA was carrying out its "'enhanced interrogation"
program, it was based around the concept of "learned help-
lessness." Make a detainee feel so dependent, so unable to control his own fate, so unable to understand it, eventually he'll

lose the will to resist, become pliable, and tell you whatever he thinks you want to hear. That's how I was beginning to feel. I was literally helpless. I was physically dependent, of course. I couldn't move, or eat, or breathe on my own. But I never would have anticipated how *mentally* helpless I'd feel.

One moment, I'd be in a room with my wife. Then I'd close my eyes for a second, and it was another day. It was 3:00 AM, after another surgery I couldn't remember, and Eric, a member of my security detail, would be there, sitting in a chair by the door. Always Eric. He always seemed to be the member of my detail on duty when I woke up at some strange, lonely hour, after a disturbing, bizarre dream, feeling like I was at the bottom of a long dark well and couldn't make noise even to yell for help, even to let someone know I was there, awake, and alone. Eric somehow always sensed it.

"Sir?"

"Eric?"

"You awake, boss?"

Eric became my stalwart, sitting upright by the door no matter what time it was. "I'm here," he'd say, and I'd be calmed for a moment.

"Eric, what time is it?"

Time was the first thing that'd been taken from me. The first thing I wanted to get back. Time was my first grasp on awareness, my first handhold out of the deep dark well in which I was stuck, physically weighed down, mentally weighed down.

Eric was supposed to be there to protect me from some kind of follow-up attack, but what he really protected me from was my own mind. "I'm here for you."

He could sense I felt better knowing someone was there

with me. So he talked to me, in the middle of the night or in the early morning, whatever time it was when I found myself awake and feeling like the only person on the surface of some cold barren planet. He spoke just to let me know he was there.

Then he was gone.

I was awake again, without remembering ever having been put under, and he wasn't there. I was left to just look at the walls. It must have been a different room because the wall had an interesting design, pictures of butterflies that looked very realistic, butterflies that, as I looked closer, I realized were not pictures of butterflies at all but actual butterflies. The wall had come alive with butterflies moving and shifting, some kind of projection on the wall maybe, then the butterflies quivered and took off. They leaped off the wall, and suddenly it was the middle of the night and Eric's voice was back. "…dream?" I heard him saying. "You had that dream again, sir? It's okay sir. It's okay."

It went on like that for an eternity. I never saw daylight. My life became a series of moments when I woke up, came out of a surgery without knowing when it started, or how long it went on, or what it was for. Only knowing that someone had been cutting and tugging and moving things around inside me.

So I prayed. Whenever I was awake, and conscious, and not completely disoriented, I tried to speak to God. I knew I'd asked for a lot already—the memory of lying on the field and praying flickered back to my mind sometimes—but I asked for more. Whenever I could think straight for a few moments, I tried speaking to God.

I'd never realized how much I relied on my mind. How much I took for granted the ability to comprehend basic facts about my surroundings. Not until it was taken away.

June 20th, 2017

My kids. Where are my kids? I'm confused and disoriented from being moved from room to room. All I want is that feeling I get when I've just come home and see Jen and the kids after a week away from them, and they run to me in the doorway and hug me and kiss me and we laugh. I want the sweetest part of being a father, the greatest part of my life. What's wrong with that? Why am I being deprived of it? Where is my daughter? Where is my son?

My voice is coming back, little by little. The breathing tube has come out, but it scratched up my throat, so I'm too weak and in too much pain to talk. With great effort, though, I can make sound. I can make a kind of forced whisper, a low growl, if I concentrate and if I'm patient.

I see Jen's face do a strange thing when I try to signal the need I have to see my children, to feel their weight on me. How badly I need to hug them. I can't read her expression.

It's been nearly a week since the shooting, and finally I'm told my kids are coming. Tears are in my eyes. There's nothing I need more in that moment than my daughter and son running into my arms and laughing. There's a knock, and the door opens, and there's Maddie and Harrison. It feels so impossibly long since I've seen them last. I'm overcome with excitement. I'm finally seeing my children, and then, just as quickly, my excitement comes crashing down.

I see it first in Maddie's eyes.

She doesn't look excited to see me. She's not smiling. She looks scared, and confused too, and now I understand, this is not her father. This person up on the bed is not the happy, exuberant daddy she knows, and I can almost hear what she's thinking, *What's wrong with him? What are all these machines doing in here? Why does he have all these tubes coming out of him?!* And poor Harrison is just standing there, stunned, frightened by his father, looking to his big sister for guidance on what to do. I'm frightening my own children.

It's in that moment, looking in my children's eyes, that I fully understand how bad things really are.

✤ ✤ ✤

And that's what it was like for a month, which sometimes felt like a year, and sometimes like a few minutes. It was a slow process of putting Humpty Dumpty back together and dealing with infections like putting out brushfires. Dr. Sava had said at the beginning: It's not *if* you get an infection, but when. I had the nose tube out; I had the nose tube back in. I was moved out of the ICU, a sign of progress; then another setback, a temperature spike, and I was put back in the ICU.

It was weeks of waking up in the dark, in a fog, slowly, slowly realizing I was in the ICU recovery room and that I must have just been in surgery again.

Weeks of waking up, and going through that slow process of trying to figure out where I was and what's happened. Weeks where I'd I try to reach through that thick fog and grab onto the idea that part of my confusion was heavy medication, so eventually, hopefully, it would wear off.

I'd try desperately to be patient about getting my mind back, and then forget why I was so adamant about being patient.

Weeks of waking up in the recovery room of the ICU and not being able to feel any of my limbs. Of being able to feel my limbs, but feeling like they were bars of heavy lead, sewed to my torso, impossible to move, but alive with pain.

Weeks of not knowing.

Not knowing if my legs would ever move again. Wondering what life would be like. Would feeling come back? Would the muscles come back? Would I ever run again? Would I walk?

It felt like too many things had to fall into place, too perfectly, for me to have any hope of ever moving again. So much was slipping away from me. A friendly face would be there, and then I'd be rolled away and wake up later, feeling like a minute had passed, and the friend was gone, because the friend had actually been there two days ago, a week ago. It felt like people were being plucked away from me, like I was being pulled away in a current from the people I loved.

It was a month of surgery, and confusion, and perhaps most of all, an intense, unabated thirst. I was realizing all the things I took for granted. The incredibly simple things, not even the ability to walk, but the ability to *think*. The ability to feel liquid. To feel thirsty, turn on a faucet, put a glass under it, take a sip, and to not be thirsty anymore. I pined for a day I'd be able to do that again. I was always thirsty. I had an intense need, and no way to address it.

Each time I complained, a nurse gave me two ice chips to suck on. Just two.

I didn't know how brutally my intestines had been shredded. I didn't realize how closely the nurses were monitoring what went in—and what went out—until I'd hatched a plot for what I thought, in my depleted, medicated state, was the perfect crime.

I woke one night with that intense thirst, and as my eyes adjusted to the darkness, coming into focus was a half-drunk bottle of lemonade. I didn't know who'd left it there, but I focused in on it. I wanted that lemonade. I could nearly taste it. I *needed* it.

"Hey," I wheezed, to a person in the room whose name I'll take to my grave. "Just hand me that lemonade. Just let me have a little. Will you? Just hand it to me. I swear, I won't tell. Just need a little."

A few minutes later, after the lemonade had been drunk and the evidence disposed of—or so I thought—a nurse came in and checked one of the tubes, and her face went red.

"What did you just do?!"

How did she know? She was keeping such close track of my body that she could see that what came out was more than what was supposed to have gone in.

My loss of independence was total. It wasn't just that someone else had control of my surroundings; someone else had control of the inside of my body.

"I'm just thirsty!"

"You can't have *anything!*"

"Why?! I am dying of thirst, and you're giving me two ice chips!" *And what about Jell-O,* I thought. *This is a hospital, why no Jell-O? And why can't I even drink water! Water is good for you!* "I thought water is good for you!"

"Not the way you are right now. It's *not* good for you. Not much of anything is good for you right now," the nurse shot back. "Making it through the next day is what's good for you."

I thought she might appoint a special prosecutor to iden-tify my accomplice. I refused to snitch, but I wouldn't have been surprised if she'd yanked the blinds and took out the jumper cables to get answers.

Still, it didn't make sense. I was dying of thirst, and hydra-tion is good. All I wanted was to hydrate, right? I didn't know that surgeons had detoured my digestive track; that even the smallest contaminant could be disastrous, could ignite another infection.

I wasn't thinking about that. I was thinking that I was uncomfortable and frustrated. I wouldn't back down, and the Great Thirst Skirmish reached a brief and fragile ceasefire only when the nurses agreed to give me something else for thirst.

Once I saw what it was, I was ready to fire up the gears of war again.

"Okay," she said, holding the least appetizing lollipop I'd ever seen. A stick with a small sponge on it, which had been dipped—barely—in water. "You can suck on this sponge."

If I had had better control of my body, I would have rolled my eyes. "This is the dumbest thing I've ever heard of."

"You can have one of these every hour," she said.

"Why? What are you doing?" *What kind of hospital doesn't let people hydrate?*

This went on for days.

I'd woken up impatient and was somehow still losing patience. I was going into a patience deficit.

But at least, in my ongoing pursuit of liquids, I was hold-ing onto a thought for more than a few minutes at a time. In a way, it was a sign of progress. Or maybe, it was helping me *make* progress. I'd found a cause, and a calling, in trying to defeat the nurses (who, I'd easily forget, were trying to keep me alive).

I was a spymaster running a deep cover asset, whose mission was to try and surreptitiously procure Arctic Blitz and sneak it past the nurse's station.

Every time I woke up, I felt desperate for something to drink, and every time a nurse came by, I launched a new thirst offensive.

In the energy with which I tackled this, though, I eventually realized, I was being given proof that I was slowly getting some of my strength back.

I was able to receive a few visitors, and I began taking phone calls, just a few. Soon I could summon enough strength in my voice that I was able to have a few short conversations. Jen had confiscated my phone and doled out time with it judiciously, careful not to let me expend too much valuable energy. Brett was at the Capitol, running my whip office during the day, so when Jen was with the kids, my district chief of staff, Charles Henry, would keep me company, filling me in on what was happening in Louisiana and sneaking me a phone call from time to time.

After a month, I was still weak, I still had a hard time moving any part of my body, and my skin was still gray and dead looking, but they let me have a "field trip." They transferred me into a giant La-Z-Boy–style wheelchair where I could be partially upright but my legs were still straight and immobile in front of me. They wheeled me out of the hospital room, and I made the great, exciting trek...to a courtyard outside.

Then, as I began to have a little more sensation in my arms, they gave me a long blue metal stick, with a circle on the end of it that looked like a dog leash, and they showed me how to use the dog leash stick to hook my foot and pull my leg, as I tried to get my feet to loosen up a little.

Another small sign of progress.

Then, I was also able to negotiate with the doctors for an increase in my allowance of ice chips.

Eventually, as a treat, I received a thimbleful of Gatorade that I didn't have to drink in secret. I nursed that shot of liquid for what felt like an hour. It was the best gift ever. It was another sign that I was taking baby steps in the right direction and the first real sign that I was moving away from imminent danger.

✣ ✣ ✣

Before the shooting, I'd tried to pray every night. It was harder now, because often, I didn't know when it was night. I didn't know when the last time I'd prayed was. I didn't know when the last time I'd been *awake* was. But it was the one thing over which I sometimes had some small level of control.

I, personally, feel a deep-rooted relationship with God, built on years of conversations, and I felt that those conversations gave me a foundation to place my burden on His shoulders; to begin to feel some peace because, even given the condition I was in, I felt that, ultimately, He was in control of my life.

But there's one part of praying that I think can actually help anyone, regardless of faith.

Part of what was so helpful to me doesn't depend on

whether you have a relationship with God or how close you feel that relationship is. When I pray, I try not to be demanding (with some obvious exceptions, like that day on the field, when I asked for just about everything). I try to remember not just to ask for things, but to thank God for all the good things that have already happened for me. Whoever or whatever it is you believe in, part of praying is practicing gratitude, and when you take stock of your good fortune, you *feel* your good fortune more profoundly. You remember it more often. You think about it. And you feel better when you're thinking about the good things in your life. Most of us are more blessed than we recognize, but we can change what we recognize.

If it seems strange that I was able to thank God when I was lying in a bed, sore, paralyzed, and feeling tortured inside my own brain—it was actually, in a way, easier at that time to be grateful. Just as my wounds were extreme, just as what had happened to me was extreme, so too was the combination of miracles that had to happen for me to survive. They were hard to ignore. They were easy to see. Sometimes, the worse things are, the easier it is to see miracles. The easier it is to recognize your blessings. No one wants to be in a bad car accident, but if you're in one, and you walk away, you see a graphic representation of how lucky you are.

That's what it was like for me. For me, praying was what New Age medicine types might call the power of positive thinking. It sounds hokey, but it's actually completely logical. Gratitude is an accelerant to health and healing. If you want to think of all the things that have gone wrong and all the ways in which you've been cheated, that's not hard to do. You suffer doubly, though. You suffer the gunshot, and then you also suffer the constant feeling of injustice nagging at your psyche.

If you want to think about all the ways you're lucky, all the gifts you've received, it can be harder. At least, at first. It gets easier though. It's actually something that gets better with practice.

And there's a simple logic that works for the believer and strident atheist alike: If you count your blessings, you benefit from them more. You enjoy eating the good meal, and you enjoy the fond memory of it later.

When you pray, you remember the things you're blessed with; you remember your good fortune. And when you give thanks for the things you're blessed with, regardless of how you do that, you amplify their impact.

July 4th, 2017

So finally, after almost a month, I was ready. I was getting better, and I was ready to be released.

I couldn't have been more excited. After almost a month in the hospital, a month of more surgeries and near misses than I care to remember, I'd started to overhear whisperings about what came next.

Jen was beginning to leave the hospital for hours on end to meet with people at the rehab hospital. I was like a child overhearing parents discussing a birthday party. I knew what was coming. Soon, I'd be released. I'd move to the rehab hospital—no more ICU rooms, no more disorienting middle of the night transfers. I'd be in my own room with constant light, and there'd be people laughing, and equipment to help me regain control of my body.

Since much of the staff at the rehab hospital was gone for the holiday, we decided to wait an extra day before I transferred over.

Still, the week of July 4th felt like almost too perfect a time for my big landmark. After having been made to feel like an attack on me was an attack on the country, what better time could there be to break free? Everyone was in good spirits. Despite some very close calls over the past month, disaster had been averted. Dr. Sava and his team had saved my life too many times to count. Through an extraordinary convergence of small, inexplicable miracles, I'd survived. Thanks to the heroism and bravery of Dave and Crystal and of Officers Jobe, Jensen, and Battaglia; thanks to the quick thinking of friends and colleagues like Brad; and thanks to a trauma surgery team on the leading edge of trauma science, I'd been given a second chance at life.

As my condition continued to improve leading up to that holiday weekend, Dr. Sava left for a vacation with his family at their lake house, and I was given time to reflect on how lucky I'd been. To consider all the people who'd come together to help me, all the hundreds of things that had to happen, the things that had to go just right in order for me to be where I was: alive, having made it through the darkest days and ready to learn to walk again. And really, when I stopped to think, it was astounding. My colleagues were beginning to say, "You took a bullet for us," since I was the only reason a security detail was on the field that day, and even that aspect of it was hard to wrap my head around: The fact that I fell in love with the Congressional Baseball Game so early on that even though members of leadership rarely make time to play, I couldn't bear to give it up, even after I became a leader.

What were the odds, really? Why did the gunman choose that specific day? A day when that gate was locked, so he couldn't get on the field?

A day when, unlike all the other days on the practice schedule, pitchers were resting their arms. Every other day, they threw in the bullpen, right there along the third baseline, so had it been any other day, the gunman would have easily picked off all of them, even if he couldn't get onto the field.

What were the odds that the first bullet would hit that chain link, knocking it just enough off its course that it missed Trent Kelly's head by millimeters?

That the bullet that hit Matt Mika's side would take an

inexplicable turn and somehow exit his chest instead of hitting his heart, so that he would survive instead of being killed on the spot?

That Officer Jobe would get to the scene at the *very moment* Dave was running out of ammo—the very moment the gunman would otherwise have had free rein?

Even if you leave aside that Brad, a doctor with trauma experience, was on the field that day, what are the odds that he would have seen almost my *exact* injury and been so haunted that he'd never forgotten it, and knew exactly what he had to do to give me a chance at surviving?

Why was that the *only* morning Brad didn't leave early?

It's not just that I felt protected by a higher power, it's that I *really* tested that higher power. We made God work overtime to get the pieces in place for me to survive.

Why did Brad have that strange change of heart that made him leave the field for the batting cage, even though he hated the batting cage, and which put him in the perfect position to see me?

What were the odds that the 911 lines would jam, and instead of slowing the response, it would speed the response up, enabling first responders to get to me even *faster*?

Why did the seas part for Richard Krimmer, every light turning green just as his ambulance got to it, the whole way to the field? How do you explain that?

How do you explain a Park Police pilot bending the space–time continuum to make two trips to the hospital in less than the time it should have taken to make one?

That the call to the trauma center came during the one part of the day when two teams were there, overlapping, so we had twice the support?

That I'd ended up not at the closest hospital, but instead at one whose trauma team was led by a man so concerned with all the complicated mechanics of chaotic life-saving surgeries that, even though he'd long been laughed at by colleagues, he'd virtually eliminated the possibility of avoidable mistakes, any single one of which could have killed me?

That I got there just in time, just as my blood pressure was slipping into "unmeasurable" territory?

How do you show up having lost almost all the blood in your body, bleed so much you need almost three entire human beings' worth of blood transfused into you, and not only survive, but have no brain damage?

There were so many things, too many to count, and as Jennifer and I sat in the hospital room, recounting each "little miracle" to one another, it was impossible not to feel extraordinarily blessed, elated almost, that by the grace of God, I was alive. My faith had never been as strong as it was then, in that hospital bed. I'd never felt a stronger connection to God than I did thinking about all the ways in which I'd been so lucky, and it was bringing my personality back. I felt my sense of humor bubbling up.

It was easy to feel good while Jen regaled me with tales of the rehab hospital. I'd have my own room with a window so I'd get to see the sun every day. They had a courtyard I might be able to go to once I'd made some progress. Jen couldn't wait for me to see it. We'd be able to go roam around outside, in a charming outdoor space with tables and umbrellas and chairs. We could eat meals out there, eat at a real table as a family, instead of all hovered around my hospital bed. That was the other thing—soon, I'd be eating regularly. And in place of the constant grimness that comes when you're ensconced in a building full of people teetering on the brink of death, I'd be in a sunny building full of progress, people moving *toward* rather than away from something, toward trying to get control of their lives again. I was going to have the chance to contribute to my own recovery. I was going to be a human being again. And as if to match my rising optimism, as I got closer to the time of my release, my medication changed too. The doctors started giving me drugs to help me get back on a normal sleep schedule, which I would need for rehab, so I was getting more and more of my mind back too.

By July 4th, I was excited. I was giddy. Kevin and Judy McCarthy were visiting, and we were talking and joking. For the first time in a while, I was making jokes and laughing. I was *laughing* again. We were joking about my trying to whip Kevin on a vote, and I took the dog leash stick I'd been given to move my foot around and smacked it against the bed like an actual whip, and we all laughed. Jen seemed to have a little less energy than the rest of us, and she came up to the bed and touched me, which was a little strange.

My mind was on progress, and the Fourth of July holiday, and fireworks, and I had that feeling of celebration, a light-heartedness I get when I'm with Jen, Maddie, and Harrison. I tried to hold onto that memory. I said, "Take me to the island!"

In the hospital room, smiles moved off faces.

"To the island?" Jen said. "What island?

"The one with the boat!"

"The boat?"

I'd been in a happy mood, now feeling just a twinge of frustration that no one knew what I was talking about.

"Yeah, the big boat."

"Are you talking about a cruise? You're saying you want to go on a cruise?"

"The boat with the band!" Why was this confusing for them?

Jen said, "You want a band to play on the boat?"

Everyone in the room was now chuckling, a little awkwardly, like I'd said a joke no one got, although I wasn't smiling. I was trying to focus. Jen was trying to figure out what I meant. It was almost like that first day I woke up, trying to make hand signals. Suddenly it was like no one could hear what I was trying to say.

"Boats with bands?" Then Jen got it. Not *musical* bands. I must be talking about *wrist* bands. The Disney "MagicBands" they give out to get into attractions. The "boat with the band" was a Disney cruise.

"You want to go on the Disney boat? You want to go to Castaway Cay? To the Disney island on the big boat?"

"Yes! You know? Our happy place!" I was using the term Jen always used.

"Okay. You want to go on a Disney cruise."

We all laughed, but Jen didn't seem to think it was all that funny. Why was Jen so serious? Why was she being such a downer? We were just having fun, but Jen didn't like that I was acting like a child. She didn't like that I'd taken a hard left turn into a conversation nobody was having.

Discretely, when I wasn't paying attention, she asked one of the nurses to check my temperature. They wheeled a big machine in, it beeped and whirred and did its thing, and the temperature came back.

Regular.

Jen was still a little uneasy. She touched me again. She thought I felt hot.

A little later, she felt my head once more. This time, she thought I felt cold. Jen was getting upset. She thought I looked flush. Jen went and got the $40 child's thermometer our pediatrician had recommended for the kids and that she brings with her everywhere she goes. She put the thermometer to my ear.

It registered my temperature as over 104.

She called the nurse.

The nurse wheeled the big machine back in and pushed the button to make it do its thing.

Again, the machine said my temperature was normal.

"I *know* what the machine says," Jen said, exasperation starting to show. "But it has to be wrong. I *really* think he has a fever."

"Well, this is an $8,000 machine. It's not wrong."

"I'm telling you it is. He has a fever. Look at him. His coloring's off. He's flush. He's hot; then he's cold. He's talking crazy stuff. Something isn't right."

One more time, the nurse wheeled the big machine in, it zipped and hummed, and again, the machine said my temperature was normal.

The nurse looked at Jen.

Jen stared back.

And then, for the first and only time during the whole ordeal, Jen decided to call attention to herself. She *demanded* attention. "Okay, well, your machine's wrong. Get another machine. This machine is wrong."

A resident who'd come into the room tried to calm things down and suggested that perhaps Jen was partially right, that things were just a little off, but that it was just me adjusting to the change in meds.

One of the other doctors on call came in and agreed. It was just the meds; don't worry.

"That's not it. This started *before* the medicine changed."

Her voice began to tremble.

"I'm telling you, y'all are missing this. I'm *telling* you."

The nurse explained patiently that everything was okay and that Jen really needn't worry. We all just accepted that Jen, who'd held it together so incredibly well for so long, was beginning to let it all get to her. She was just a little paranoid, that's all. And who could blame her, given all she'd had to deal with?

Besides, if ever there was a time for Jen to not be on top of her game, this was it—when I was finally through the woods and she no longer needed to be the one person keeping the family together, me together, and our world from collapsing.

It was understandable, and of course totally forgivable, but Jen was losing her cool.

✢ ✢ ✢

That night, the kids wanted to go see the big fireworks display on the National Mall. Jen didn't want the kids anywhere near big crowds. She felt they deserved a distraction, though, so reluctantly, she decided to let them go with a babysitter.

Not good enough.

"We want *you* to take us!"

She looked at our children. As much as she dreaded the

idea of being in a crowd herself, she felt that with all the energy and attention she'd been devoting to me, she'd neglected the kids. I told Jen she should go with them. She should be with them doing something fun. I knew it wasn't the most comforting idea for her, but it'd be good for the kids to get out and take their minds off the hospital for a bit.

Jen put on a brave face and set off for the fireworks display.

With my wife and kids away, as it got closer and closer to the time the fireworks were supposed to begin, I started to get confused.

Where was my family?

Why was my family abandoning me on the Fourth of July?

I had the TV on in the hospital room, all ready to watch, and they were nowhere to be found.

As the fireworks began on the TV, I called Jen, and I made my voice sound agitated so she'd know I was disappointed in her. "Where are y'all?"

"We're at the Capitol!" It was noisy on the other end of the line. "The fireworks are going off!"

"Yeah I know the fireworks are going off. I'm watching them on TV. I thought y'all were going to watch with me."

"No, no. I put the TV on for you to watch, but I'm with the kids at the Capitol."

I was getting angrier. I wasn't sure at whom. Maybe at Jen.

Over by the Capitol, Jen hung up the phone after our conversation and shook her head. "Something's wrong. Something's wrong." Jen sees me as the "World's #1 Dad" and tells people she's never seen me prioritize myself over our kids. My outburst of what sounded like selfishness and impatience was (to her) too out of character to let slide.

After standing with the kids and thinking for a moment, she said, "We have to go back to the hospital. Sorry kids, we have to leave." To herself, she thought, *Something's not right. I don't feel good about this.* By the time they were back on the road, Jen was in such a rush she wouldn't even take a seven-minute detour to drop the kids at the hotel, and when she got back at the hospital, Jen found me looking dazed. She thought I looked like a zombie. She used her pocket thermometer again. This time, it said I had a temperature of 104.1.

She pressed the nurse button. "He has a high temperature. Look!"

Another nurse came in to see what was going on and, if only to appease Jen, examined me. As she did, Jen leaned over and said quietly, "Look how hard and distended his abdomen is. He's getting more delirious. I really think something's wrong."

The nurse looked back at Jen.

"I think so, too."

✣ ✣ ✣

Steeled by her new sidekick, Jen approached the doctors and steadied her voice. "I don't like it. Y'all need to do an x-ray or something. Whatever it is. CAT scan. I don't know. But some-body needs to look on the inside. It's not right. I'm not leaving until somebody agrees to take another look. Okay?"

Later that evening, they finally relented.

After going back to the hotel with the kids for a few hours, Jen came back to the hospital the next day knowing an x-ray had been done but not knowing what the results were. A nurse she didn't recognize was standing by the door of my hospital room, as if guarding it.

Who's this?

The nurse introduced herself as part of the hospital's Rapid Response Team, on alert because the x-rays on me had shown an air pocket. An air pocket was a sign of infection.

A few minutes later, Dr. Sava called. This was a surprise. Dr. Sava was supposed to be on vacation. Jen didn't know it and neither did I, but he had been checking in on me remotely, talking with his colleagues still at the hospital, even while he was out at his lake house. He'd heard Jen had been upset about something, and he'd come to feel she had as acute an eye for my condition as anyone.

"Jennifer," he said over the phone, "talk to me. Tell me what you're seeing."

"He's not right and no one's been listening to me." She was still angry and still worried. She didn't feel vindicated. She was now worried that whatever was happening was worse than everyone realized. "Dr. Sava, it's *not* just the medication. He started the new medication *after* I started seeing this... erratic behavior. He's delirious. His abdomen is extremely distended. Something's not right. He's gotten worse every day since you left."

"Jen," Sava said over the phone, "Jen, listen to me. Tell me what his temperature and his heart rate are."

Jen recited my vitals over the phone. She tried to remove desperation from her voice, but the truth was, she felt she needed Dr. Sava there, as the one she knew really trusted her gut. "When are you coming back in town?"

"I'm going to come back tomorrow."

She felt a little better after talking to Dr. Sava. He was on top of it, and he very obviously trusted her observations implicitly, but she still wished he could be there. She would never tell him that, because she also felt that he deserved time away with his own family, having been so dedicated to ours for so long. But she couldn't help herself from feeling that we needed him there.

A few hours later, unprompted, she got a text from him. "I'm on my way."

He'd changed his mind. "I'll be there in a couple of hours."

And right around then, Susan Kennedy, assistant director of the trauma department, walked into the room, having just seen the latest test results. She had a serious look on her face.

"What?" Jen asked. "What is it?"

"He's going back up."

Jen knew what that meant.

"Up" was up to intensive care.

Behind Kennedy, a team marched into the room, took hold of the bed, and wheeled me away. It turned out a juncture where part of my digestive tract had been stapled was leaking and had been for long enough that, by that point, I was in sepsis. I was going into renal failure. My kidneys were shutting down.

By the time the sun rose on the day I was supposed to finally be free, finally released from the hospital, I was back in intensive care, fighting for my life all over again.

I was back to square one.

The Gunman

The day before the shooting, a home inspector named James Hodgkinson—at the time living near a baseball field in Alexandria, Virginia—called his wife to say he'd be home soon.

Hodgkinson had for a long time been a kind of hyper-engaged citizen. He was engaged in his community in an Illinois town just across the Mississippi River from St. Louis, Missouri. He was a man with strong beliefs, stubborn when defending them. Back in grade school, his friends knew him as a fun-loving kid, vibrant and energetic. He was on the smaller side, but he was an athlete; he wrestled and ran track. He played pick-up baseball with friends.

After high school, he became a small businesses owner, running a construction company for two decades and then changing it to an inspection company, doing air quality testing and home inspections. But at some point, something in him changed, or perhaps he'd always had a very dark side and it was only a matter of time before he let it emerge.

The biggest change in his life came in 1996, when Hodgkinson and his wife took in a foster child. The child had been a ward of the state for 12 years, her biological parents having forfeited their right to care for her. To Hodgkinson, she seemed levelheaded enough to perhaps thrive, in the right circumstances.

It turned out, though, that he didn't know everything about her. She had deeper demons than he knew, and one day, they overtook her. His new daughter got in a car and drove south out of the city, pulled over onto the side of a remote, rural road, poured gasoline all over her body, and lit herself on fire. She died out there, alone.

After his foster child took her own life, Hodgkinson learned something that made it even more devastating—that this wasn't the first time she'd tried. She'd made at least one attempt before, but her history of suicide attempts had been withheld from him.

It'd be irresponsible to say this was a turning point that caused his life to go off the rails; we don't know, and I believe it's at least as likely this was just a horrible bump on a road he was already on. What I know for sure is that I wouldn't wish this tragedy on my worst enemy and, also, that suffering a tragedy, no matter how inconceivable, does not make someone cause others pain. That was not inevitable. It was something in him, a decision he made, to hurt other people.

And not just my colleagues and me.

He tried once more to be a foster father, and while at least this time no one died, it again ended in disaster. He had a great-niece whose parents were delinquent, too—another child who'd been in and out of foster care. Hodgkinson and his wife agreed to take her in, to become her legal guardians, and she even took their last name. She was 12 by the time it all became official, right around the time many children are just about to show their rebellious side, and Hodgkinson, it turned out, was ill-equipped to handle a teenager.

Within a few years, as his adopted daughter began asserting her teenage independence, Hodgkinson began losing control. Of her, and also of himself. He proved unable to contain a rage that was rising in him.

It seems that around 2006 a truly violent side began

to emerge. He was trying to get his daughter home from a friend's house, but she wouldn't come. Hodgkinson went to get her, things escalated, and whatever it was that had been brewing inside of him, for however long, broke through. He snapped. He grabbed the girl by the hair and yanked her to the floor. She got up and, with a friend, sprinted out to a car to try and escape, but Hodgkinson ran after them, pulled open the car door as she tried to pull away, took out a knife he had, and sliced the seatbelt off of her. The friend screamed that she was going to call the cops, and Hodgkinson punched her— punched a teenaged girl, a child really—in the face.

After that, tensions cooled briefly; everyone went home, but it seems that this was the moment a genie was released from a bottle it couldn't be put back into. You cannot un-hit a child. He'd proven to those around him, and perhaps most importantly, to himself, that he was violent. He'd shown himself to be the kind of person capable of violence toward a child.

When the girl's boyfriend showed up to confront him, Hodgkinson pulled out a shotgun. He hit the young man in the face with it, and when the boy ran, Hodgkinson shot at him.

Later, a judge stripped Hodgkinson of guardianship but placed the girl with next-door neighbors, so Hodgkinson was reminded, just about every day, of what he'd done.

✣ ✣ ✣

In 2008, Hodgkinson found a new outlet. He began writing letters to the editor of his local newspaper. It was a stint in which he was a sort of old-fashioned, engaged citizen. He dropped his opinions off at the *Belleville News-Democrat*. He paid attention to how people responded. He engaged respect-fully with rival viewpoints, for a while at least. Over time, though, he grew frustrated, and his civility started to break down. His anger emerged. He began to shout in those letters. He attacked powerful people he disagreed with, but he made almost bizarrely technical points, citing percentages and tax brackets, getting way down into the weeds. His letters read like university economics assignments, full of lists of percent-ages and brackets, discussions of "top marginal tax rates" and different ways of measuring government revenue. He would read economics books and then cite their lessons to the other letter writers he was arguing with. He name-checked trea-sury secretaries from decades ago and went through their hits and misses. He was animated by the arcana of tax policy, like very few people are. He sent almost 30 letters to the editor at his local paper in the span of just a few years.

And then his new passion for political expression inter-sected with the 2016 presidential election cycle, and every-thing spiraled out of control. He'd become an outspoken Bernie Sanders supporter, volunteering on his campaign, and it was a blow when the Democratic establishment threw its weight behind Hillary Clinton. It was a bigger blow when Trump won the election. Hodgkinson went into a rage. On social media, he hurled profanities at Trump and joined groups dedicated to terminating the Republican Party. He grew angrier and angrier. He let his business license lapse, so he was now unemployed, a full-time political flamethrower, with little to distract him from his own anger. It fed on itself.

By the spring of 2017, he seemed to be irretrievably gone, set on his course, and there was just one last chance to stop him.

That March, one of Hodgkinson's neighbors heard what sounded like bullets being fired. The neighbor thought they were .45 caliber, the noise was so loud. When he looked out the window, he saw Hodgkinson, holding a rifle up to his shoulder, aiming at something, pulling the trigger, again and again. Hodgkinson shot dozens of rounds, apparently just at trees, terrifying the neighborhood. Sheriff's deputies arrived and confronted him, but there was nothing they could do. Hodgkinson had a valid gun license. Though he'd terrified his neighbors, he was shooting on his own property. It was clearly very unusual and upsetting, but it wasn't illegal. The deputies filed no charges. They asked him to shoot responsibly and let him be.

A few days later, he left for Virginia.

✤ ✤ ✤

For a few months, he had a strange little existence carved out for himself. Since he was near Washington, D.C., he took time to visit the sights. He visited the Supreme Court and the Library of Congress. He went to a tax-themed protest. He went to the National Mall and walked around the lawn—the same lawn I saw every day at work when I looked out of my office window.

He watched golf and drank beer at a local restaurant, where he kept to himself. He avoided eye contact. Some days, a woman working behind the bar tried to engage him, but he was quiet. She thought he had a strange smile.

At night, he retired to his cargo van.

In the morning, he took a gym bag out of the vehicle, went

to use the showers at the YMCA, and sat in the gym's reception area, whiling away the hours on his laptop.

On Tuesday, June 13th, he called his wife. He used the Wi-Fi for a while, posted a political cartoon to his Facebook page, and when he looked up from his laptop, he could see, not even 60 meters away, the main baseball field at the Eugene Simpson Stadium Park, where we were all practicing.

The next day, he attempted one of the biggest political assassinations in the history of the United States.

July 13th, 2017

A strange thing had started happening, beginning all the way back when I first lay unconscious after the shooting.

Everyone, it seemed, wanted to *do* something. First, it was just being there. They were led by Cedric, who managed to find out what hospital I was at and to get there before anyone else, straight from the Democrats' practice and still in his baseball uniform.

Then more of my colleagues came, and more. The president arrived. So many people converged on the hospital to see me, even before anyone knew how serious it was. The hospital was crowded with people wanting to know how I was doing, trying to wish me well.

Then it expanded.

As the media began correcting earlier misinformation and reporting that I was actually in critical condition, all around the country, people started to reach out. Close friends and strangers alike. People started asking Jennifer how they could help. The first thing she thought of was blood. I'd lost so much blood; I needed 20 units from the blood bank just to make it through that first day. She started telling people who asked how they could help to organize blood drives. Back home, my friend Jeb put one together at our church, St. Catherine of Siena, and they had "Scalise Strong" tee-shirts made for people who donated.

My alma mater, Archbishop Rummel High School, partnered with Ochsner Medical Center to hold a blood drive in the school gym, and they gave out shirts too. Soon, there was news of blood drives being organized all around the country.

Churches started organizing prayer groups.

America was mobilizing.

The Democratic speaker pro tempore of the Louisiana state house organized a blood drive in my name, and people from both sides of the aisle showed up to give blood.

On the Tuesday after I woke up, Inova Blood Donor Services held a blood drive in the Rayburn House Office Building next to the Capitol, organized by my friend, Chief Deputy Whip Patrick McHenry. Vice-President Pence came by, visited with my staff, and donated blood. In Washington, D.C., Republican and Democratic members of Congress turned out to give blood. It didn't seem to matter to people what my politics or my religion was. People wanted to help. Over the next days and weeks, all over America, people leapt into action. This is what America is about. This is what America does. People brought out the very best in one another. Many different people, from all different backgrounds, joined together for this one cause. *E pluribus unum:* Out of many one. People organized numerous replenishment drives on my behalf, giving blood at their local Red Cross chapters, at churches and high schools and Kiwanis clubs.

People began sending messages that they were praying for me. People who believed in my God, and people who believed in others. People who didn't believe in anything.

I learned that on the day of the shooting, Cedric and the Democrats had all immediately gathered to say a prayer when they heard the Republicans had been attacked and that I'd been shot. I started hearing, more and more, people say things like, "I'm praying for you" or "My mom is praying for you" or "My kid's school group is praying for you."

I swear, I could feel it. Even before they told me. Not immediately, not all at once, but as I woke up and became slowly more aware of my surroundings, those thoughts and prayers *mattered*. Even the ones that came from people I'd never met before. Maybe *especially* from people I'd never met before. Each time I woke up after a surgery, disoriented, in an unfamiliar room, with a different kind of pain and confusion, there were dozens more cards and letters. I was being connected to people all over. There was a huge, powerful wave of positive energy following me, focused on me, no matter what strange place I woke up in. All of these prayers were giving me strength.

I never lost faith, but those were days that tested it, days that drained most of my optimism. What kept me from bottoming out, what revived me, in an almost literal sense, were these gestures that connected me to people all over the country.

I couldn't quite comprehend why people were taking the time to do it and what it meant, and to be honest, I still don't totally understand, but I do know those prayers got me through some of my darkest moments. Every time an infection set me back, every time the projected date of my release got delayed again, every time Dr. Sava had to deliver disappointing news, there were people there to cheer me up. Sometimes it was my closest friends who showed me I wasn't alone. Sometimes it was powerful people who visited. Vice-President Pence stopped by several times; the speaker of the House came as well; the president and first lady were at the hospital on the very first night. The king of Jordan sent a giant bouquet of flowers and a letter. The prime minister of Israel, Benjamin Netanyahu, called the day of the shooting, and when I finally woke up, we spoke on the phone, the two of us sharing a very personal conversation, one that moved me deeply.

At the U2 concert I'd planned to attend in D.C., Bono, for some reason, took it upon himself to tell 49,000 fans at FedEx Field, "We're so grateful that Congressman Scalise and his comrades made it through. . . . We hold them up as love holds us all up," even though he had no way of knowing I was such a big fan. And while he was in D.C. for the concert, Bono came by my office in the Capitol, signed a get-well card for me, and took pictures with my staff to cheer them up. When I woke, I got to speak on the phone with him, too. I was able to tell him that I was supposed to be at that very concert and that his prayers had meant the world to me. I relived some memories with him. I told Bono how I'd seen him in the mid-80s on the riverboat *SS President*, which went up and down the Mississippi River. Bono laughed.

"That was *way* before *Joshua Tree*; I remember that!" he said. "You really are an old-school fan!" He invited me to be his guest at the next concert in New Orleans (which I ended up having to skip because of yet another discharge date being moved back).

My alma mater, Louisiana State University, had made me an honorary coach for the College World Series and dedicated the first pitch to me. Then they took the ball from the first pitch, signed it, and the next day had it hand-delivered to me at the hospital by my friend Scott Ballard, a member of the LSU Board of Regents.

The Chicago Cubs came to Washington, D.C., for a visit to the White House to celebrate their historic World Series win a few months earlier. After the ceremony at the White House, one of the owners, Tom Ricketts, who I'd seen literally days before the shooting at an annual gala for the World War II museum back in New Orleans, came to the hospital to visit. He didn't come empty-handed though. He came carrying the World Series trophy! That 30-pound piece of sterling silver was coming down the hospital halls on the way to my room!

These were the kinds of uplifting moments that brought smiles to my face and occasionally tears to my eyes and helped, in the lowest moments, to keep my spirits strong.

✤ ✤ ✤

More often, though, it was a letter or a call from someone I'd never met that pushed me along. The notion that a stranger would take the time to pray for me and cheer up someone they'd never met moved me, and it strengthened my faith in humanity after one deranged man had shaken it. There's something very powerful about learning people are thinking about you all over the country. That all over this great nation, people are focusing their positive energy on you. It's like beams of light coming through dark clouds, and so even while I lay mostly paralyzed in that hospital bed, hurting all over, it felt like I was glowing.

Whenever I reached one of the most frustrating moments— when I was dying of thirst; when I was desperate for a sense of routine and woke up in a different room with some different part of my body cut open; when I was asked to perform the simplest task, just to lift my arm, and couldn't; when I wondered if I'd ever leave, ever see the sun, ever be able to walk, ever hold my children again—whenever one of those burdens felt like it was about to topple over and bury me, I'd be handed a card from some far-flung place. The card would explain how someone was thinking about me, or the senders would tell me how their children had told them they hoped the man from the news got better. It would make me feel like I *had* to get better, for those strangers, and that I *would*, because of them.

One woman crocheted crosses and mailed them to me. Another knitted me prayer blankets. I'm Catholic, and the number of relics and bottles of holy water that showed up was staggering. People with late-stage cancer told me they were praying for *me*. Brad Wenstrup, who'd already saved me once, told me his young son said, unprompted, "Daddy, we were just praying for your friend." And though sometimes people wonder, does it matter? I mean, can you really feel it when someone prays for you? My answer is simple and direct. Yes, you can. I could absolutely feel all those prayers.

And I feel now how ironic it is and, in a way, how wonderful, that an act of madness led to so many acts of kindness. Those people reminded me just about every day why I love this country. They made me eager to get back on my feet, and to get back to work.

✤ ✤ ✤

I'd never needed those gestures more than I did on that day I thought I was finally done with my interminable hospital stay, and it turned out, I wasn't even halfway through.

The night after Jen finally convinced the skeleton crew something was wrong, after Sava came racing back early from his vacation, I underwent an emergency surgery. After that, I was back in the ICU; my condition was downgraded from fair to serious. It wasn't only that I was no longer being discharged; I was moving in the wrong direction. A week later, on July 13th, I had to have another major surgery for a deep tissue infection, and again, it was like I was back at square one, like a terrible game of Chutes and Ladders—a bit of progress, then a slide back to square one. Would I ever get out?

It began another month of being in and out of major surgeries.

Another month of long stretches without food.

Another month of not being allowed to drink, of having to recruit moles to get anything more than a few drops of water.

Another month without being back at home in Louisiana with Jen and the kids.

Another month spent languorous and confused, not knowing whether I was waking up from a surgery or just waking up from the pain, not knowing who'd done what inside me.

Another month without starting the physical therapy I so desperately wanted to start.

Another month of doing very limited pull-ups from my bed, recruiting visitors to help with exercises to stretch my dwindling leg muscles.

I was trying to be optimistic, but I was also a little wary of optimism, because the last time I was optimistic, I'd been crawling toward a mirage. I relied, ultimately, on the kindness in letters from hundreds and hundreds of strangers to pull me through, even more that second month than the first.

✛ ✛ ✛

Finally, a month after that latest devastating setback and the series of infections that followed, I was ready again. Ready a second time, to leave the hospital and begin rehab, to finally begin moving *toward* something, toward getting my life back, rather than away from death.

This time, it was real. No more infections were waiting around the corner to test my faith. I slipped through, before any complication could reach out and yank me back to the starting line again. Once at the rehab hospital, it would be up to me to work toward getting better.

And it turned out, I just wasn't ready. I had no strength.

By then, I'd lost 50 pounds. I'd lost the entire weight of my son. Over almost two months of rarely getting to eat real food and hardly moving, my body had atrophied. (Before the shooting, it's true, I could have stood to lose a few pounds, but this was definitely not a weight loss plan I recommend.) All the muscle had melted away or constricted into tight, weak little knots. Even a feather of pressure on my feet shot daggers up my legs, because my calf muscles had tightened so much that they felt like stones. I knew I'd been lucky that no nerves had been severed. No major nerves had been transected despite all the shrapnel flying around in my body, but still, nerves get stunned asleep by the trauma of projectiles zipping by them, and you don't know whether they'll wake up or not. My body was a rigid, atrophied wooden board, knotted up, tight, weak, and useless. My only hope was going to be building up some strength to compensate for the parts of me I still couldn't move. I needed to get stronger.

If I was going to have any hope of getting stronger, I was going to need to find a way of putting a whole lot of weight back on.

July 20th, 2017

THE CHEF

On the morning of the shooting, my friend Tommy woke up at 6:30 AM to get ready to head into his restaurant. He carried his cell phone into the bathroom and closed the door gently so as not to wake his wife. He put it on the vanity, turned on the TV he has in the bathroom tuned to the local CBS affiliate, and started his shower.

On the bathroom vanity, his phone started buzzing.

When he stepped out of the shower, he saw his phone had lit up with missed calls and messages. He reached down to pick it up, and a call came in from his brother, at the same moment the CBS affiliate broke in with a special report.

Tommy was still dripping wet as he listened with one ear to what his brother was telling him, and listened with the other to the correspondent on TV. "Did you hear?" his brother said. "Steven's been shot." As if to confirm, the correspondent on the TV said that the congressman from Louisiana's first district was among those wounded during a shooting at a baseball practice in Virginia.

At 7:13 AM local time, 8:13 AM Eastern, just as the trauma team was prepping to race me from the trauma bay down to the operating room, along with a phalanx of officers in tactical gear, Tommy texted Jen. "Please let me know if you need anything."

Fifteen minutes later, even though he knew Jen probably had a hundred calls and text messages, Tommy texted

228

her again. He wanted Jen to hear from him. "Sweetheart my prayers are with you, Madison and Harrison," he texted. "Please give them a kiss for me."

✥ ✥ ✥

Tommy wasn't the only Louisiana native who would end up being there for me in a big way, not by a long shot. South Louisiana is like one big family, everyone looking out for each other. But in choosing one example to show how incredibly and how creatively people showed up for me, there's perhaps no better person than Tommy. Tommy is the epitome of a Louisianan, from his salty sense of humor, to his larger-than-life personality, to his taking-it-a-little-too-far New Orleans school spirit (when he goes to his kid's high school games, he roots *against* their school and *for* their crosstown rival, because that's where he went), to the way he represents perhaps our proudest export—food. Tommy's a chef.

Tommy's father, Drago, was the embodiment of the American Dream: a Croatian prisoner of war who immigrated to the United States and started a restaurant that ultimately became one of the biggest and best seafood franchises in New Orleans, Drago's Seafood Restaurant, employing over 500 people. Part of the company's success comes from Drago's grit and work ethic, but a lot of it comes from one particular innovation of Tommy's.

It was right around the time Paul Prudhomme, a Louisiana native and arguably America's first celebrity chef, had popularized a new way of preparing a fish almost every fisherman, until then, threw back. Prudhomme invented "blackened redfish," which became a craze, and every Cajun seafood restaurant worth its salt served a version. Drago's served a version, covering the fish with a butter garlic sauce and cooking it "on the half shell," which meant you left the skin and the scales on half the fish, to serve as a trap, keeping all the natural juices and bastings in.

That was on Tommy's mind one day in the kitchen, while over at the oyster bar, the operation whirred along, workers shucking and plating, shucking and plating.

And suddenly, the two things fused in his mind: Everybody in seafood always talks about oyster water, how it's the best broth nature ever produced.

And everybody was cooking blackened redfish in a way that kept the fish's natural juices and broths in.

So, what if you cooked an *oyster* that way?

What if you put an oyster on the grill and prepared it like everyone was preparing blackened redfish, using nature's best broth?

Tommy mixed up a sauce, poured it on a shucked oyster, threw it on the grill shell down, moved it around to account for hotspots, let it all cook from underneath, tried it, and thought, *Damn, this is good!*

Soon charbroiled oysters were on the menu. But the moment Tommy knew he had a commercial hit on his hands was when, after a meal, it came time for a customer to choose from the restaurant's decadent dessert menu and the customer said, "You know what? For dessert, how about just another dozen of those oysters?"

Tommy says he was just fooling around and got lucky and came up with something that now pays for his kids' tuition and all his bad habits. It's also how he came up with what, in my opinion, is the best single bite of food in the world. The first food, and to be honest, one of the very first things, I thought of when I woke up in a daze after being shot.

✛ ✛ ✛

On June 14th, as the day wore on, the news Tommy began to hear about me changed.

It began to get much worse.

First, he'd heard, like everyone else, that it was minor, a shot in the hip, I was doing fine.

Then he heard that maybe that wasn't quite the whole story.

Tommy decided to fly up to D.C. so he could be there for me. A big brother instinct kicked in. He didn't think there was much he'd be able to do, but he felt if he could say something funny or off-color to Jen and get her to crack a smile, then the trip would be worth it. He took a 5:00 AM flight the next day and arrived at the hospital by late morning. He didn't get to see me that day, but the more he heard, the more worried he became. He tried to keep his feelings secret from Jen, but once he heard the path of the bullet, he started to fret. *Man,* he thought, *you got the intestines. You got your stomach. You got your abdomen. You got your kidneys. You got your liver. All that shit's down in there.*

Every new piece of information Tommy heard devastated him. He felt as if it were his own body. He returned to New Orleans a few days later, wondering if he'd ever see me awake again, feeling certain that if he did, I wouldn't be the same person.

Back in New Orleans at the restaurant, Tommy was trying to keep himself from obsessing over how I was doing, but it'd been days since he'd had an update. When Jen's phone number showed up on his screen, he was actually excited, eager for information, anything. And he knew what his role was. He made his voice as bright as he could for Jennifer. "Hey, sunshine!"

But instead of Jennifer, a male voice came on the line, scratchy and low, almost a whisper.

It was me. Trying as hard as I could just to form words. I'd woken up only hours before. My throat was still mangled by the breathing tube. I could barely whisper. But among the first things I'd thought about after waking up was Tommy and, believe it or not, those oysters (maybe not in that order). The only thing I could manage to say was a low, strained, raspy, "Hey, buddy."

For a minute, for the first time since I'd known him, Tommy was speechless.

I'd never doubted how deeply Tommy cares about my family and me, but if I had, that conversation, brief and strained as it was, and as hard as it was for me to even get enough air going to form a word, would've put any uncertainty to rest.

After collecting himself, Tommy, close to tears, said, "That is the best thing I've heard in I can't tell you how long."

✛ ✛ ✛

As I was being transferred to the rehab hospital, I couldn't have been more excited. It was such a huge milestone for me, something I'd been looking forward to for what felt like ages. I couldn't wait.

Then I got there and realized how weak I was. How much weight I needed to put back on, how much strength I needed to get back, if I was to have any hope of learning to walk again.

Tommy, it turned out, had just the thing to help. He was revving up for what I'm pretty sure were the greatest morale boosters in the history of convalescence. At least for a Louisianan.

Tommy knew how starved I'd be for the food New Orleans is famous for, so he'd gone back to where it started for him: the kitchen. He planned out a meal—trout almondine, seafood gumbo, and, of course, most important of all, charbroiled oysters—and began organizing a feast. He texted Jen. "I land in D.C. at 10:00 AM tomorrow. Get me some Crisco, some milk, and an address where I can meet you."

Jen knew right away what he was mobilizing for. She tried to convince him that traveling to prepare for one meal was too much.

"Screw it, no," he said. "I'm coming up to cook for my boy."

And he did. Tommy flew up to D.C., this to cook a few of my favorite dishes. He invaded the kitchen in the apartment Jen and the kids were now renting; the kitchen must have seemed like a tiny closet compared to the industrial kitchen he was used to working in, but he made it work. When he was done, Tommy came by the hospital to deliver the meal, and he saw Dr. Sava hanging around. Sava still hadn't entirely let me out of his sight, even though I was in rehab and no longer his responsibility. Tommy liked that. He saw how some of the doctors and nurses and therapists were so committed to me. How genuinely they seemed to care about their patients.

That gave Tommy another idea.

Why not cook for them too? Why not cook *at* the hospital? Why not try to brighten up everyone's day a little?

Drago's didn't have any locations outside of the Gulf states, but why not bring the whole operation to D.C., into the hospital, if only for a day?

Once he'd decided to do that, he turned into a bull. *I'm coming, and I'm cooking. Make it happen.* There was no stopping him. He called the hospital's kitchen manager to tell (not really to ask) him to arrange the space, and then back in New Orleans, Tommy sat down with his restaurant managers to go over everything they would need, as if they were a special forces unit planning a raid. The Drago's kitchen staff laid out all the equipment—the skillets, knives, burners, everything Tommy didn't trust someone else to provide—and Tommy picked out his favorites. For the few things he'd need in D.C., he texted instructions to Jen.

"You're gonna need to have the oil, and bread for dipping."

Everything else, he packed. Tommy and the restaurant managers put all the equipment into suitcases, threw in a couple of gel packs to keep the ingredients cold, sealed them up, and set out for the airport. Tommy flew up to D.C. yet again, this time laden with bags of restaurant equipment and ingredients. He got to the rehab hospital, laid it all out in the courtyard, and got to cooking.

People started emerging from the hospital to see what was going on. The dietician came out, and the hospital's chefs stood next to Tommy at the grill. Tommy began teaching the secrets of Louisiana cooking, the secrets that had made Drago's restaurant famous. The hospital chefs couldn't believe they were getting a chance to learn from a Cajun food legend.

They couldn't believe their luck—but Tommy was happy to share his secrets, because he wasn't there just for me. He was there for all the people he'd seen taking care of me. He wanted to cook for them, too. He couldn't bring them all into his restaurant to show his appreciation, so he turned their place of work into one.

I was wheeled out into the courtyard, and Tommy began handing out paper plates loaded with the very best Louisiana seafood, made fresh, by hand, right there at the rehab hospital. It was funny, and delicious, and amazing. It was Tommy's way of communicating through food his appreciation to the hospital stuff for taking care of his boy, and his way of trying to lift my spirits.

It did just that, at the most important time. Just as the high of moving to the rehab hospital was starting to fade, just as I was learning how weak I was, especially on my rebuilt leg, which I still wasn't even allowed to put weight on, Tommy had come and put a smile on my face.

A few days later, back home in New Orleans, Tommy got a text from Jen.

"Steve had a checkup with his orthopedist today. We got the good news...he can start doing more aggressive PT on the left side."

I was getting my strength back, I'd suddenly got my *leg* back, and I swear, it wasn't a coincidence that it came right after a sudden infusion of charbroiled oysters!

August 10th, 2017

Once I started eating again, after I was finally discharged from the hospital and transferred over to begin my rehab, I realized just how much I'd craved routine. Just having a schedule. I was no longer worried about everything being turned upside down. I was no longer waking up in strange places with sedatives fogging up my brain.

Now, I woke up every day in the same room. I wasn't worried about people barging into my room every couple of hours to take vital signs and poke and prod my latest incisions. I'd craved being able to go to sleep with confidence that I'd wake up in the same place, after a full night without interruptions. Now, I had a room. A window, with sunlight every day.

I had food. Of course, I'd missed food as much as anything else. My taste buds came back alive. Fried Chicken Tuesdays, that was enough to learn to walk for. Grits in the morning. Meatloaf that wasn't half bad. My diet had been ice chips and weird sponge lollipops, which doesn't exactly fill out the food pyramid, with a side of whatever was pumped in through my feeding tube. It's no wonder I'd lost so much weight.

My body had started to heal but was still broken. Sometimes you sprain an ankle, and it hurts to put weight on it. Sometimes, you simply lose control of parts of your body, like I had on the baseball field. When you try to move, nothing happens. And sometimes you can feel the signals getting to the right body part, but that part of the body is too weak to move. It's like the motor's revving, but you're in the wrong gear. The tire's stuck in mud; you can't get moving.

I had all three of those problems—pain, partial paralysis, and extreme weakness. We had a lot of work to do.

It was clear that if I was going to have any hope of learning to walk again, it was going to depend at least as much on my upper body as it did on my legs. My legs were nowhere near ready, but my upper body had atrophied too. My abdomen had been cut open, sealed, and cut open again, more times than I could count. My abdominal muscles had been treated like a zippered sweatshirt, opened and closed, opened and closed. I didn't have the strength to sit up in bed by myself, and when I tried, I had searing pain.

My whole upper body was useless, and what made that so frustrating was that I simply had not known all the things that had been wrong with me. I think the doctors deliberately withheld some information I was now learning, because there are certain things so severe, so out of the patient's control, it really does no good to tell them until the patient is through the woods.

It was only when I was in the rehab center, trying to get my body back, that I learned how badly my intestines had been shredded, how totally my pelvis and femur had been pulverized, about all the rods and pins and what sounded like spare automobile parts that had been plugged into me in the hopes of one day maybe getting me back upright.

So for a while, it wasn't just that nothing worked, it was that I didn't understand why nothing worked. I was shot in the hip. What did that have to do with my stomach muscles? Why didn't my stomach muscles work? Why were my arms so weak? Why did I have so much pain in a leg that wasn't even shot?

I wasn't close to getting my legs to move. In rehab, they'd say, "Lift your leg a little," and I'd try, and we'd watch to see if anything woke up, and nothing did.

My arms were in no condition to carry the weight of my body. I was only just getting to the point where I could lift them up at all, but even that was a chore. It took tremendous effort. The muscles didn't want to respond; it was as if they were rebelling.

So, we started small. Therapy, at first, was in my bed, and I just lay there and let the therapist work on me. My physical therapist, Meaghan, and my occupational therapist, Mandy, would be my guides (and godsends in their own right) in the weeks ahead, helping me relearn the most basic tasks, tasks I'd always taken for granted. But at that point, all I could do was lie there, as they stretched and kneaded my leg, trying to get the muscles to loosen.

Then they lifted me out of the bed, put me in a wheelchair—not an oversized La-Z-Boy, but an actual wheelchair, a downgrade that felt like an upgrade—and rolled me to the physical therapy room with all the equipment. That was progress. I was getting to move again, even if it was only when someone pushed me.

Then I got to the training floor and was reminded of how little progress I'd made.

They had to train me how to use my body all over again, and my body was working against them, especially my calf muscles. Even after 15 minutes of trying to knead them into relaxing, they were so tight from disuse that when my foot grazed the ground it felt like knives shooting up my legs. It was pain like I'd never experienced before, the kind that makes the corners of your eyes wet and scrunches your face up before you even realize it. And this pain wasn't even in the leg that had been hit by the bullet.

When I recovered from the stabs of pain, we began. We began by just trying to relearn the most basic tasks. The things I'd need to know if I wanted to be even remotely self-sufficient again. Since I still couldn't move my legs and I couldn't bend at the waist, I had to learn to use a set of gadgets to put on my shoes and socks: a grabber, a hook, and a long shoehorn. All these long tools to fuss around with my feet, like I was stoking a fire I couldn't get close to. It took days before I made any progress, and even with those tools, I couldn't get my shoes on or off by myself.

Then, in the middle of the night, I woke up with sharp pain in my ankles.

The next night, it happened again.

The night after that, it was worse.

Finally, the doctors recognized the problem: The muscles in my ankles were so weak they couldn't even hold my feet up. Over night, gravity pulled my feet down to the sides. I was slowly, every night, respraining my ankles. They had to fashion fiberglass boots to keep my feet upright when I slept. They surprised me by making the boots my school colors, one purple boot and one gold, but I'd been shown that I couldn't even *sleep* without hurting myself. Even doing the thing that is the absence of doing a thing was setting me back! I had a long way to go.

✛ ✛ ✛

If I brought one thing to the project of trying to get back on my feet—a task for which I depended mostly on other people—it was patience. Things would work out, however long it took. There was no going back.

I believe that patience comes from faith. I've always felt God has a plan for us, and I felt that more keenly after the shooting. You have to find a way to believe things will get better, eventually, even if there's no evidence of progress. Even if there's no apparent reason they should get better. If someone says, "Move your leg," and you try, and nothing happens, there really aren't a lot of options. There's no "Let me try that differently." If the connection isn't there, if some synapse isn't firing, if your nerves aren't communicating, there's nothing you can consciously do about it. You just hope that maybe tomorrow, things will start working. That maybe tomorrow, whatever nerves were dormant today will wake up on their own.

My problem wasn't just the weak muscles I was trying to build back up. It was also nerve damage, and I couldn't fix that just by trying hard. All I could do was wait, not give up, and have faith that, eventually, God would make sure things began to work again.

For as long as my body didn't work, all I could do was to take that discouragement and try to isolate it. Let it happen, let myself be disappointed, but try to keep it from leaking into the tasks I actually had control over.

If the only part of my body I could control was my right arm, well then I'd build that right arm up so strong I'd throw a better fastball than Cedric.

If the only thing I could control was my right leg, I'd get that one strong enough to kick a 60-yard field goal.

I was in pain, and I felt like I had forever to go, but I seized on what I had. I still had a team of people around me dedicated to getting me on my feet. I still had people sending prayers from all over the country. I had members of Congress stopping by to tell me that people in their districts were thinking of me, were praying for me.

I had Jen holding everything together. I was getting to see the kids more and more, and the kids were seeing their dad get a little better each day. Just spending time with the kids, seeing them at peace, seeing them comfortable with me, no longer afraid, that gave me incredible strength, the kind of strength any parent can relate to, especially one who, like me, didn't get to see his children very often for a long period of time.

I had routine. I had that room. I had a window and sun. And I got to wake up in the same place every day. That meant I had a foundation. And it meant that even though I was supposed to be learning to walk and couldn't even move my legs, I was getting my mind back.

Perhaps most of all, I was eating and I had the right to choose what I ate. I looked at a menu, and even if there were only two or three options, *I* was the one controlling what I put in my body. So it wasn't *just* that I was getting to eat again (though of course that was a huge part of it). It was that even if I couldn't move much of my own body, the act of looking at a menu and making a simple choice like whether to have Jell-O or pie for dessert was proof that I was starting to regain control over my life.

✢ ✢ ✢

I was also slowly taking control of other things. Jen had been with me, keeping our world from collapsing, for two months.

She'd put her life on hold to make sure the children didn't have to put theirs on hold and to make sure mine could go on. She was a godsend. In several specific ways, she saved my life, as she did in other, harder to define, but just as significant ways.

She also took something from me, though. Something very important, arguably the key to a happy, fulfilled, productive existence in this life—my cell phone.

She refused to let me have control over my own phone for nearly two months, worried that I'd exhaust myself working. She worried (probably correctly) that whatever store of energy I drew from to recover, I'd run it dry returning phone calls and text messages if given the chance.

I, however, desperately wanted to get back to work. I knew that my new, normal schedule and this new life in which I made decisions, controlled what I ate, and worked hard in physical therapy was providing me a sense of agency that was power-charging my batteries. If I could get my phone back and begin checking in with the office just a little more frequently, just poke my nose back into my work life, I thought I'd recover even faster. Or maybe I was just impatient and trying to justify it. Either way, on August 10th, I had my chance.

Jen flew home that day so she could get the kids ready for school. It was the first time she'd left D.C. since the day of the shooting, and it was the beginning of a new, brutal schedule for her—she began flying back and forth every week so she could be with me in D.C. and be a mom in New Orleans, too.

On that day, when she left, she gave my phone to Brett for safekeeping.

The next day, down in New Orleans, Jen's phone beeped with a text message. It was from me. All it said was "Surprise!"

Followed by no fewer than 13 smiley face emojis. She counted them.

Instead of calling me immediately, she called Brett.

"Brett, are you kidding me?! I leave for ONE DAY! You caved!"

"I'm sorry Jen! He signs my paychecks!"

Jen laughed. "Yeah, but you know what? I can have you fired too!"

I laughed too. I was coming back. We were now having lighthearted moments together, and in a way, my little act of rebellion was a milestone. We were all *laughing* together. We weren't worried any more that I was potentially moments away from a life-threatening infection. There was a new lightness. So cell phone in hand, I began inserting myself back into life as majority whip. It did feel like therapy, to feel useful again. That may have been because when you call someone from a hospital, you tend to get to yes much more quickly. We had a budget coming up, tied to a big tax overhaul—complicated, controversial legislation tricky for many members—but when I called members from a recliner in the hospital, that resistance tended to dissipate quickly.

Soon I had staff coming to get work done in the hospital, and not just Brett. You could see the therapists and doctors looking quizzically at each other as a gaggle of men and women in suits marched into the hospital every few days like accountants doing a surprise audit. One of my doctors told me I had to take at least one day off of work, since I'd taken on a seven-day-a-week schedule. I said I'd consider it.

✜ ✜ ✜

As my mind got stronger, slowly my arms got stronger too.

I got to the point where I could go to the gym and lift weights. Pathetically low weights, but I didn't care. I could lift *things*, even if they only weighed a pound or two.

Soon, I'd be ready to take on another big milestone: being upright. And though I hadn't expected to come back from the shooting and start running wind sprints, I *had* expected that I'd remember how to stand up.

I didn't.

Part of the problem was that my brain had forgotten all the things it used to do automatically. The part of the brain that does ballast control—that runs in the background, tensing and relaxing muscles in your body to keep you upright when your center of gravity shifts—that part hadn't been used in two months. It's supposed to do those things automatically. You're not supposed to have to think about it.

I had to think about it. I didn't know how to balance. It was like trying to teach someone how to breathe or speak his native language. You don't actually remember learning how to balance, you just could always do it, as long as you can remember. That makes it hard to learn it again.

And what made it even harder was that I was trying to balance a completely different body. Two months earlier, I was stronger, heavier, and both my legs had the same range of motion. Now, my right leg was weak, my left leg didn't move, and every muscle in my body was tighter, weaker, and less tensile than it had been before I was shot.

So, we started with two parallel bars under my arms,

just trying to remember what it was like to be in an upright position.

Just a few seconds at first were all I could manage before the strain on my arms and the pain in my leg became too much to bear.

The next day, though, I held myself upright for just a little longer.

The day after that, a few seconds more.

The progress was minuscule, almost unnoticeable, but not quite. I noticed. I stood up for five seconds. Two seconds more than the day before. I rejoiced.

For the first time, I was having measurable success. Even if it was extremely modest, it was something I could take pride in. Something I could thank God for. I'd survived the shooting because of the bravery of some heroes, the brilliance of others, miracles I had no control over, the attentiveness of Dr. Sava, the presence of Brad on the field, God looking out for me, and all the other things people did to save me. For the first time, I was being given the chance to feel like I was contributing to the enterprise of my recovery.

Some days I got to see Crystal at the rehabilitation hospital. Though her injury hadn't been life threatening, it had been serious. Her entire ankle was shattered. Crystal's an incredibly strong woman, but she had a lot of rehab to do to get back to work and to get back to her life. And though I hated the fact that she had to be there at rehab like me, I can't deny that it filled me with joy every time I got to see her. She brought a smile to my face every time we ran into each other (or, more accurately, were wheeled past each other). She'd give me a fist bump. She'd whisper a joke or some small word of encouragement, and it would motivate me for the next training session.

When Jen was there with me, Jen would try and give Crystal an extra boost, and when Crystal's wife, Tiffany, was there, she'd give me some extra inspiration, too. Our two families supported one another. As patient and understanding as the staff at the rehab hospital was—and they were extraordinary—the one, thin, silver lining to the fact that both Crystal and I had been shot was that our families could give each other the kind of support that can really only be passed between people in the trenches together.

At least, I know Crystal and Tiffany gave that to me.

✣ ✣ ✣

For the time being, my main goal, my highest aspiration, was to stand up. All I wanted was to stand.

I made it to 30 seconds upright before my grip on the bars weakened, my arms gave out, and Meaghan needed to support me.

I made it to 40 seconds standing up, under my own power.

The next day, I made it to 45.

The day after that, I sprained my ankle, and it was back to square one.

I'd pushed too hard.

For the next week, I had to work just to get back to my previous 45-second record. It doesn't sound like much, but when your arms are quivering from the strain of keeping your body upright and your only point of contact with the ground is one leg that doesn't even really feel like your own leg, 45 seconds is an Olympic record. A few sessions each day with my physical and occupational therapists were paying off, and I was a (not quite) walking example of "no pain, no gain."

After another week, with great effort, total exertion, and no small amount of pain, I could stand on one foot, with my hands clenching the bars, for an entire minute. The road was still very long, but I was moving in the right direction. Even if I wasn't, actually, literally, moving yet. Still, I'd made enough progress that the therapists started adding bonus challenges. That was the reward I would get from Meaghan and Mandy for showing signs of progress: even harder tasks.

Now it wasn't just standing up; it was standing up and trying to balance while I pulled little plugs out of little holes in the wall and then put them back into other holes. Like those old games of Chinese checkers, but vertical. I had to reteach my body how to account for the kind of subtle shifts in weight that happen when you reach an arm out to shake someone's hand or take something out of the fridge. I had to rebuild muscles I couldn't name and had never heard of before. I had no idea how critical your glutes were to standing and moving.

Soon, I was ready for another task: not walking, exactly, but a clumsy approximation of walking. I still had no use of my left leg, so I'd hold my weight up with my arms, just like before, but with my weight loaded onto my hands, I'd try and kick my right leg a few inches forward. I'd slowly transfer some weight onto that leg, shimmy my arms forward until they were over my foot, and then swing the leg forward again.

After a few days of doing that for an hour and a half twice a day, I had enough strength built up in my arms and my one working leg to take a few, small, pained steps. Then I wanted to begin testing out what it was like to put weight on the other side. I had a trip across the street to see some of my medical team, and Dr. Golden, the orthopedic surgeon, looked at an x-ray and said, as nonchalant as if he was asking me to pass the salt, "You're cleared."

"I'm *what?*" He was saying I was ready to put weight on the leg that had been shattered by the bullet. It had healed enough. "How much weight? Twenty percent? Thirty?"

"A hundred percent. If it hurts, stop. Your body will tell you how much you can take. But otherwise, go for it."

I couldn't believe it. After all the tiny, incremental steps, and then the giant setbacks, this was now a giant leap forward. It meant I had all the pieces in place. It meant I was ready for the next big milestone on the road back to walking again, to use a machine I'd been looking at during every PT session, with great anticipation, for weeks.

✢ ✢ ✢

The first time they attached me to the ZeroG Gait and Balance machine, I felt like I was being strapped into an F-16 (which I actually got to do a few months before, but that's a story for another day). The engineering of that balance machine felt almost as awe inspiring. The harness was attached to a winch, connected to a sort of robot that looked like an upside-down spider, crawling along the ceiling above me on a track. Strapped into the machine, I looked like a grown man in a Baby Bjorn, except that the straps didn't hold me in place or keep me from moving. Instead, the spider robot crawling above me could pull on the straps to "unload" my weight, which just made me feel like a lighter version of myself. That way, I could relearn the mechanics of moving without as much strain. I pushed along on crutches, while above me, the robot followed. It was like the marionette, and I was the puppet, dangling below.

When the robot sensed I was starting to lose my balance, it tightened the cables, just enough to keep me upright. In the moments I was maintaining balance on my own, I could almost imagine the robot wasn't even up there above me, except for the fact that I felt lighter.

All along, it was recording. How far I walked, how much support it had to give me to keep me upright, how many times it had to kick in to keep me from falling. All of these metrics helped me track those little bits of progress.

✛ ✛ ✛

My spirits were now higher. I went back over to the hospital to meet some of the people who'd helped save my life and let them know I was back on my feet (sort of). At least, I was getting there, and I had a bunch of stats and metrics to prove my progress. It was a special experience because I'd been in such a fog the whole time I was there, in and out of intensive surgeries. There were so many people who'd helped me but I'd never met, or at least couldn't remember meeting. And one whose life I made miserable while she was trying to save mine: I met the nurse who rationed the number of ice chips I could eat, the anti-Gatorade tyrant, my thirst tormenter.

I remembered her vividly, just as you remember the person who haunts your nightmares. She came over when she saw that I was doing well. We made fun of each other, she ridiculing me for being such a stubborn patient, me ridiculing her for being a medical professional torturing her patients. But when we had a quiet moment, I could tell she was emotional, seeing I'd made it so far. I was too. In that moment, I apologized for making her job harder. And I thanked her. I thanked her for being one of the many, many people who saved my life.

August 25th, 2017

The rehab nurses and occupational therapists started giving Jen pointers for the things she'd need for showers, baths, entryways, everything. How to modify bedrooms and bathrooms so I could get around. They fitted me for crutches, and my response was Pavlovian. I was like a dog seeing its owner grab a leash and the keys. Crutches had to mean I was getting out soon.

Jen, unbeknownst to me, had started daydreaming about ways to surprise me, to mark the occasion of my release, while I began daydreaming about how, when the time came, I was going to make my comeback.

✢ ✢ ✢

I couldn't just show up back at the office. That wouldn't do. It was important, really, extremely important, for me to find some way of acknowledging all the people who'd come together to help me. The people who'd done very specific, heroic, exceptional things to save my life: the doctors and nurses and Capitol Police detail, the Democrats and Republicans in Congress who'd shown so much support.

Not *only* them, though.

I felt like I needed to use my return as a way to thank *all* the people, all over the country. All the people who'd prayed for me, sent crocheted crosses to me, sent holy water to me, organized blood drives in my honor, and gave blood in my name. That had been such an incredibly powerful thing, and it was going to be difficult to express in words what it had meant to me, this power being sent into my hospital room from all over the country. I'm generally an optimistic person, but it wasn't just some kind of inner strength that kept me from slipping into darkness and depression and self-pity. It was hundreds of people, thousands of people actually; it was you. I have dozens of binders in my office now, binders full of handwritten letters people sent me. I wanted people to see how much that had meant. How it had reminded me, again and again, of why I had to get better, why I *would* get better. How Americans had constantly reminded me of how good people can be.

You reminded me of that. And I needed to return the favor.

Since nothing I said could possibly convey just how appreciative I was, I knew I needed to do it in gestures. I decided there were two ways I'd do that. The first was choosing the right way to come back.

We thought about having some kind of official event back home in Louisiana, before my family, friends, and constituents and some of the folks who mobilized so quickly to do what they could for me. It'd be a good way to celebrate Louisiana, as the perfect symbol for all that's good about the country as a whole. No one deserved my gratitude more than the people of all different colors and creeds and affiliations around New Orleans. They were some of my first heroes. A Louisiana comeback would be heartfelt. We all liked that idea.

And yet, I couldn't shake the idea that if I had a comeback celebration in Louisiana, I'd be giving up part of the message I wanted to send. People from my home state were a huge part of my recovery, probably the biggest part, but it wasn't *just*

Louisiana. It was all of America. How could I make sure that I reached everyone?

I decided I was making it more complicated than it needed to be. My job, after all, happens to be in a building whose very purpose is to represent all The People. Why not just do it there?

But that still left the question of *when*.

Speaker Ryan offered me the opportunity to address my colleagues on the House floor during a vote series. That made the most sense: Because there were so many signs of unity throughout my recovery, I could share that moment with all of the people who played such important parts in my life over the past three and a half months. Plus, since House proceedings are carried live on C-SPAN, my friends from back home could watch, and I could have a place for Jen, my staff, and other members of my new extended family in the House gallery.

That left just one last problem. It happened to be the biggest one of all. Could I actually pull it off?

With everyone watching, could I walk, under my own power, from my office, down to the chamber, and up to the lectern?

I didn't want to use a wheelchair. I wanted everyone to see that they'd helped me get back on my feet. And I'll admit that I wanted to show that I—really, that we—had triumphed over violence, that good had conquered evil.

✤ ✤ ✤

We decided to keep my return date a secret while my staff mapped out how exactly we'd do it. If I was going to pull this off, it was going to have to be carefully planned and expertly executed. It was going to take a lot of help from a few trusted people. And it was going to take a lot of luck, too.

At first, we told only the people who absolutely had to know. Back at the Capitol, while I was finishing my last few weeks of rehab, Brett slowly started cluing in the few people who would be involved in my return, a handful of staff from the speaker's office, the sergeant at arms, and a few members of my own team.

Then Brett got to work figuring out a route to the House floor from my office. It was a trip I'd made a hundred times before, without ever having to give it a second thought, but that now required detailed advanced planning. Before the shooting, I took the steep spiral staircase to my office, two at a time, racing my security detail. I wasn't quite ready for that yet. Brett started actually doing the walk himself, finding different routes, counting how many steps each route took. He walked out of the office, down to the speaker's ceremonial office, into the chamber, all the way up to the lectern where I'd give the speech, and back, counting silently to himself.

It was too long. It was just too far. Brett didn't like it. I'd never make it. I'd exhaust myself before I even got to the lectern. What if I fell? What if someone had to hold me up, to keep me from collapsing? Even if I *did* make it, what if I was panting so hard by that point that I couldn't even speak without huffing and puffing? I'd only just started using crutches a few days before.

Another thing I hadn't thought of is that the House Chamber slants up. It wasn't just the distance that would exhaust me; it's actually an uphill walk to the lectern. At that point, I was only barely able to take a few steps under my own power, and that was on even ground. Going uphill wasn't just more tiring, the mechanics were different. I still couldn't move my left foot; I had to use the rest of my body to whip my leg around and steer that foot into place. That was all going to change if I had an upward slope to deal with. I'd only just figured out a way to take a few steps in my new body. Now I had to figure out another way.

Added to that was something new that had begun to weigh on me. Maddie's school holds a father–daughter dance every year, with a photo booth and a DJ, and it had always been a highlight of the year for me. Of course, at the dance, the girls spend most of the night hanging out and dancing with each other, while the dads are the wallflowers, waiting patiently on the outskirts of the dance floor, catching up with each other and waiting for our turn. There's always at least one moment where, perhaps out of guilt, the girls work their way over to the dads and we get to have one cherished dance to some new pop song. It's a blast, and it's heartwarming and something I'd come to cherish. Sometimes, you don't realize just how precious time with someone you love is until you don't have it anymore. I was thinking a lot about that as the day of the dance approached. It sapped me of motivation, to know I wasn't well enough to do this one simple thing I'd always looked forward to. Just when I was beginning to get into a rhythm of constant progress, I was reminded of how far I still had to go before I could ever approach the life I'd once had.

Jen and Maddie, it turned out, had come up with an idea. If I couldn't go to the dance, they'd bring the dance to me. They'd planned it all out with the hospital staff, asking if there was a room they could take over and turn into an imitation school gymnasium. Maddie ditched her friends and flew up to D.C. They even set up a makeshift photo booth, just like they had at the dance. If Maddie was disappointed that she wasn't with her much cooler friends, she did an Oscar-worthy job of hiding it, and instead of the father–daughter dance, we renamed the event the Maddie–Daddy dance. We laughed, and sang, and danced, or sort of danced—since I still couldn't walk, Maddie pushed me around in a wheelchair while we played her favorite music. We watched a movie and ate sushi, one of the foods that, for whatever reason, maybe because Jen and Harrison don't eat it, has become a Maddie-and-Dad tradition. It was, in the end, an incredibly special night, an emotional one for me, our own little two-person father–daughter dance in the hospital.

✢ ✢ ✢

Later, I realized, Maddie had given me an idea, too.

The room they found for our little party was a small auditorium used for presentations and lectures. It happened to have a slight slant, just like the floor of the House of Representatives. I realized that this might be just what I was looking for; that room just might serve my purposes.

I talked to the physical therapist, we came up with a plan, and soon, after hours, that auditorium turned into my own personal practice facility.

Thanks to my 10-year-old daughter, I'd found my imitation House of Representatives, and thanks to Brett, I knew exactly how many steps I needed to be prepared to make.

My physical therapy sessions became a job of transposing,

in my mind, the floor of the House of Representatives onto that small hospital auditorium. I took my crutches over to the auditorium, pushed through the door, up the aisle, all the way to the very back of the auditorium, counting out the steps, and then I tried to stay on my feet and talk.

I practiced hiding how hard I was breathing. I tried to keep my chest from heaving up and down with the effort. I tried to keep my voice from sounding clipped and strained.

I'd stand up there and count three minutes, the next day five, then back down the aisle to the stage, and out the auditorium door.

Again and again, I did that walk, alone in the auditorium, trying to learn my new gait, trying to build up stamina.

Every day when I finished physical therapy, I'd find out if the auditorium was being used, and if it wasn't, I'd do my routine. Walking up, stopping, bracing myself, counting the minutes I could stand under my own power without exhaustion showing, without pain showing on my face, then walking back down.

All the while, I was beginning to daydream more and more, and those daydreams were dominated by two things that made me press even harder. The first was a picture I had in my mind, becoming clearer and clearer, of finally leaving the hospital and going back to Louisiana, walking back into my home with Jen and the kids. Walking. Walking into Drago's and getting that first order of charbroiled oysters. The idea that I might, one day, get to do that was as exciting as the idea of winning the lottery.

The second image I had was of returning to work and giving that speech on the floor of the House.

I dreamed about it. I fantasized about it. I was the kid in the yard pretending to score the winning touchdown in the Super Bowl, the winning run in game seven of the World Series. I was training for that moment. I spent every spare moment I had practicing.

Not practicing what I was going to say—my press team wanted me doing that, even though we all knew if I made it through that long walk and up to the lectern, I'd be too emotional to read a speech. Plus, that's not my style anyway. For this moment, for what I wanted to convey to everyone, I knew I'd wind up feeling the need to speak from the heart. If I ever got to that point, I'd probably mostly just emote. I'd be winging it.

What I practiced was actually walking.

The crutches were big and cumbersome. I had to build up my endurance. If I could get that gait down well enough that it was second nature and build up enough stamina, then maybe, just maybe, I could make the long walk with everyone watching. But then, as I was on my way back to my room one of those days, I saw one of my guardian angels. Crystal was there that day, speeding along in her recovery.

I noticed that she had different crutches than the ones I'd been assigned. I had "axilla crutches," the long wedge-shaped ones that go all the way up into your armpits. Hers were different. They only came up to her forearms. Maybe it was just because she's a better athlete than I am, or that she was further along in her recovery, or just the nature of our different injuries, but she was moving much better than I was. I asked her about them, and we shared notes.

She liked the crutches she had, and watching her with

them left enough of an impression that I made a note to ask the physical therapist about them later. The therapist told me the "forearm crutches" Crystal had were harder to use and harder to balance on. You couldn't just drape yourself over them like the ones I had. You needed more upper body strength. You needed better balance. My upper body was getting strength back, but slowly. Those muscles still had a long way to go after the months I'd spent in bed. Those crutches would be worse for me, in almost every way.

The one advantage they might give, though, caught my ear—the nurses said that those smaller forearm crutches, if I *could* figure out how to use them without falling, were actually more maneuverable. Since they were smaller, they were lighter, and they were less likely to get in the way. That, in turn, meant they were better over uneven terrain. They were better—and here's what sold me—for inclines.

In other words, they'd be better for climbing up to the lectern in the People's House.

Whatever it took to learn how to use the "advanced" crutches without falling over, I was going to do it. I wasn't about to return to the House floor on some kind of scooter. I was going to *walk* back to my seat in the People's House. I was determined.

September 28th, 2017

THE PEOPLE'S HOUSE

Getting my fancy new crutches was like getting a shiny new bicycle for my birthday.

I went back up to the hospital auditorium to go through my practice routine with my new equipment. Twisting my torso, swinging my left leg past the crutch, dipping my upper body just a bit, so my left foot hit the ground somewhere in front of me.

Left crutch down, right crutch down, right foot down, upper body whip, then here comes my left foot swinging around....

I was determined to master my swing-wobble so it would be second nature by the day of my comeback. I tried it out in the ZeroG gait machine (still an F-16 flight simulator to me), honing the precise mechanics of my new quadruped wobble.

Then I tried the new gait back up to the auditorium, handling all the weight myself, slowly spidering my way up the aisle.

As I made progress with my new brand of walking—and slowly built the stamina I'd need—Brett was coming up with his Grand Bargain. He knew I wanted to walk onto the floor of the House, that I didn't want to use a wheelchair, but he was convinced there was no way. It just wasn't possible. He was growing more and more concerned that if I tried, I'd exhaust myself before I even got to the chamber.

Or worse, I'd exhaust myself *after* I got there. I'd hurt

myself in front of all my colleagues. I'd fall on national TV or become so out of breath I'd be left panting into the microphone. Brett steeled himself for a fight with his boss.

✥ ✥ ✥

The afternoon of my release, with Jen by my side, I signed my discharge papers, and then, under my own power, gripping my forearm crutches, I walked out of my room. What an amazing feeling, after months of surgeries and a grueling rehabilitation, to be walking all on my own. I made it almost all of the way down the hall before needing the wheelchair, and then we headed to the Capitol Police vehicle waiting outside to take me to freedom.

Brett watched me walking down the hall; having been so busy back at the Capitol getting ready for my return, he hadn't actually seen me on my new crutches yet, and he'd missed all those practice sessions. As he watched me making my way down the hall under my own power, I could see his face changing. You could almost hear what he was thinking: *It's September, not so long after the shooting. He couldn't even move for months; today, he's walking out of the hospital on crutches, and tomorrow, he's going to nail his return.*

We had a small gathering that evening on the rooftop of Jen's apartment building with some people from the medical team and a few members of my staff who'd been doing such an incredible job not only supporting me during an intensive rehabilitation but also keeping my congressional offices running. We recapped the summer, we visited and caught up, and then we got down to business: We huddled to prepare the precise choreography of tomorrow's return. At that point, most of my staff didn't even know my comeback would begin in less than 24 hours.

Everyone was given a minute-by-minute plan of action for how the day would go, a plan that laid out exactly how we were going to get me into the building and all the way to the lectern without running out of gas.

Critically, the plan also included how we were going to do it in secret without anyone seeing me. It was going to be an emotional day. We didn't want me to get mobbed by press and use up all my energy speaking to them. I'd need every last ounce of energy I had if I was going to actually pull this off.

Plus, we kind of liked the idea of having the return be a little surprise for everyone.

After we'd talked through the plan a few times, Jen said, "Okay, now I've got a surprise for you." She disappeared for a minute, the roof got quiet, and I could have sworn I heard the LSU fight song.

The next thing I knew, I saw Jen riding up to me on a purple and gold motorized scooter! She'd had it painted the colors of my alma mater, Louisiana State University. It had an LSU Tigers decal and a purple basket on the front with the tiger logo on it. Brett had a Louisiana license plate made for the back that read "MAJ WHIP." The seat had a decal with a fleur-de-lis–shaped eye of the tiger, and the scooter turned on and off with a key attached to a Raising Cane's keychain. And the LSU fight song? That was a musical horn she'd outfitted the scooter with, which could also play "Eye of the Tiger"!

I beamed ear to ear as she rode the hot-rod scooter around the roof. It wasn't something I'd be ashamed to ride around in; it was something I couldn't *wait* to ride around in. And it would eventually take on a mythology of its own, even earning its own nickname. People started referring to my new ride as the "Go-Kart," except—and by now, this shouldn't surprise you—we made sure it was spelled the French Cajun way. Which is, of course, the *correct* way.

We called it the "Geaux Kart."

✛ ✛ ✛

The next day, we followed the plan.

We left the apartment and rode up North Capitol Street. I had a perfect view of the Capitol dome as we inched through the morning traffic, a moment to prepare myself for what was to come.

Then, we sprang into action.

We pulled into an empty underground loading dock we'd discovered a few days before, away from the press and anyone else who might recognize me. As far as we could tell, no one saw us.

Step one, check.

Now for the hard part.

Bart Reising, who handled operations for my office, along with Brett, had worked with the sergeant at arms to map out a route through the basement that would give me the best chance of remaining unseen.

It still wasn't a great chance though. The Capitol corridors constitute a maze of utility tunnels accessed daily by hundreds of workers, who keep the 200-year-old building functioning around the clock. Making it through unnoticed would require some more minor miracles. If we were going to have a chance, we had to move fast.

I motored the Geaux Kart down the back halls at top speed, zooming around corners and opening her up down straightaways before anyone had the chance to see me or try to find out what that *whirring* sound was. Brett and Jen ran behind the scooter, trying to keep up with me.

I turned a corner to ride down one of the most exposed corridors, a long open stretch with nothing to hide behind.

I held my breath.

The hall was empty. Not a single person.

I hit the throttle.

Almost home free.

At the end of the hall, I pulled into an elevator that would take us from the basement up to the second floor. The elevator door dinged closed. We started ascending, then stopped at a floor before ours, and as the doors began to open, Brett, Jennifer, and my security detail instantaneously crowded the front of the elevator to block me from view and make the elevator seem fuller than it was. The look my detail gave the waiting passengers said it all: *No room. Catch the next one.*

The doors shut.

The elevator lurched upward again.

Now, we were on the second floor, just feet away from where I needed to be. I rolled out of the elevator, made a sharp right turn, and we were there, in the privacy of the speaker's ceremonial offices. I'd made it! I'd probably broken some halls-of-Congress speed limits, but I'd made it to the privacy of the speaker's ceremonial offices without being spotted.

Or so we thought. Just as we were congratulating ourselves for our flawless execution, Brett got a text message from a reporter. "Can you confirm Scalise is in the building? I have it from someone he was seen in a basement hallway." We checked Twitter. Nothing there yet, but if I'd been seen, it was only a matter of time before word got out. It was time for me to break my silence, or someone else was going to do it for me.

Just off the speaker's ceremonial office is a balcony, affectionately called "the speaker's porch." With Jen at my side, I crutched out onto the porch and looked out at the National Mall, a similar view to the one from my office. It was a windy, crisp day, a beautiful day really. As Jen and I stood out on the balcony, one of my press aides snapped a picture, and we posted it online with a simple caption:

"I'm back."

Then, for a moment, I took to the couch in the speaker's ceremonial room to catch my breath, to go over the speech I knew I'd probably be too emotional to read, and to spend just a little time with Jen, sharing memories about the summer, and taking stock of how far we'd come. And as I sat there, Jen next to me, speech in hand, I could hear, from a TV in a room nearby, CBS breaking the news of my return.

✣ ✣ ✣

Just like that, it was time.

I kissed Jen as she headed up to the gallery, handed my speech to Brett, put my arms into the sleeves of my crutches, and got myself up.

I crutched into the hallway and made my way to the speaker's lobby, just off the House floor, and the House sergeant at arms, Paul Irving, led me to the doors of the House chamber.

I felt exhilarated just looking at the doors. I'd thought so long about this moment, and now, it was here. The doors opened.

But there was no noise.

The normal din of the House chamber during a vote series was missing. It was actually very quiet. It sounded like a completely empty room. Except it wasn't an empty room. It was filled to capacity. My colleagues were all there, my family and friends were up in the gallery, Paul Ryan was ready in the speaker's chair—all of them were waiting, quietly, expectantly.

I lifted my crutches and moved over the threshold.

✦ ✦ ✦

The moment I actually stepped into the House chamber, the silence broke open and the room roared.

They were all on their feet. I'd never heard the room that loud; I'd never heard *any* room that loud. To think, this wasn't a stadium full of kids screaming for a football team or rock band, but a room full of my friends, many of whom I hadn't seen in months, a room full of congressmen and -women all whooping and hollering like rowdy sports fans. It was incredible; the entire House chamber joined together in a roaring, cheering, standing ovation! Without even thinking, I smiled as big and broad a smile as I've ever smiled. I couldn't help it; I couldn't *not* smile. People started coming up to me as I made my slow spidery way along the floor. People were hugging me;

friends were giving me big bear hugs, weren't even thinking that they might knock me off balance, and I wasn't even thinking about balance—for the first time since I tried to stand on those first days of rehab, I wasn't *thinking* about balance; I was just watching this sea of faces, the entire House of Representatives standing and roaring, and I felt myself being carried along by them. No longer was I wondering whether I'd be able to make it up to the lectern or if I'd be winded when I got there. All I could think about was how unreal this felt, how incredibly special and how lucky I was to be alive, how lucky I was to be able to witness this.

Before I knew it, this sea of cheers and laughter and roars and hoots and hollers had carried me up to the lectern. It felt like a split second and I was there. I didn't even register being tired. I didn't register pain. I didn't stumble or trip. The wave of energy and warmth in that room from people who were supposed to be constantly arguing against each other had picked me up and carried me to my place behind the lectern. My roommates, Shimkus, Brady, and Paulsen, were right there waiting; the majority leader, Kevin McCarthy, and my chief deputy whip, Patrick, were in the seats just next to them.

And then there was Cedric.

Cedric and I looked at each other. He made a face like he couldn't quite believe I'd made it, and then he grabbed my hand and yanked me in for a hug, as if maybe this whole moment was a mirage and he didn't want to let it slip away. All around me, as Cedric and I hugged, the house still roared. It was the embodiment of what I'd felt all along, but captured in one moment, in one place—all this energy directed at me, *willing* me to get better, which I'd felt almost from the moment I'd woken up in intensive care.

As the cheering finally began to settle down, Speaker Paul Ryan finally tried to bring the House to order. He banged his gavel on the dais.

Then with a big, almost mischievous grin on his face, Paul announced that, "The chair wishes to mark the return to the chamber of our dear friend and colleague from Louisiana, Mr. Steve Scalise," and the room roared all over again.

"Our prayers have been answered!" He boomed, as if this wasn't the House of Representatives but an old Southern tent revival. Then he got serious for a moment.

"His bravery and his family's strength have been such an inspiration to this House and the people it serves. America is grateful for this moment. The chair now proudly asks"— and at this point his mischievous grin returned, bigger than before—"for what purpose does the gentleman from Louisiana seek recognition?"

Both sides of the aisle laughed, and I, caught up in the moment, yelled back, a little too loudly, "To speak out of order, Mr. Speaker!" I couldn't help it; I laughed too.

"The gentleman is recognized for as much time as he may consume!"

✤ ✤ ✤

And then I was home. The old-school Southerner came out of me, speaking from the stump, speaking from the heart, ignoring the speech that had been so painstakingly put together for me, determined to exploit the speaker's permission to speak for as much time as I could consume. I wanted to show how truly, genuinely thankful I felt toward everyone involved in my recovery and to remind everyone listening that my return had been made possible by the grace of God but also by the strength they'd all given me.

As I spoke, what I'd hoped might happen was happening: My colleagues seemed to feel that my being on my feet reflected something important about them and the people they represented. On the day of the shooting, Speaker Ryan had addressed the House. "An attack on one of us is an attack on all of us," he'd said. I was made to feel in those crucial days that that was absolutely true, that's how everyone treated me; but if we'd all been attacked, then we were also all responsible for the comeback. My colleagues had closed ranks around me, and this wasn't just *my* return, it was a return for the whole House. So I just started thanking people. For what felt like just a few minutes but actually stretched on toward half an hour, I thanked everyone I could think of, everyone who'd helped get me to that lectern. I brought up the thousands of acts of kindness and love and warmth that had come from the men and women in that chamber, as well as across the country and around the world. I told them all how much those gestures had mattered, that they were responsible for the motivation that proved crucial in getting me through each dreary day in that hospital, each grueling hour of physical therapy.

As I spoke, people watching on C-SPAN started calling and texting. Brett's phone chirped to life, and when he checked it later, he had messages from all over the country.

Friends in Chicago: "We're watching your boss on the news!" A cousin in Baton Rouge: "We're in the grocery store. Everyone just stopped what they were doing and froze; they're all staring at the TV above the checkout counters!"

If there'd ever been any doubt, we all knew then that we'd picked the right way to come back, because while many of the people to whom I owed my life and recovery were in that room, not all of them were, not even close. The fact that we could let people beyond those walls see my comeback was important to me. It was one part of the way I'd planned to signal, to as many people as cared to know, how they'd been part of my comeback.

The other part is this book.

This book has been my way of trying to continue what I started from the lectern that day. It's my way of trying to show just how many different people, from just how many different walks of life, were responsible for my being able to stand up and walk under my own power again.

This book has been me trying to show you how many miracles had to happen for me to have this second chance and how many people played parts in those miracles. It's me trying to explain just how much those prayers mattered, how powerfully I felt them. Some people did extraordinary, almost spectacular things to save my life, some made small gestures that to me felt powerful, sent letters, gave blood in my honor, prayed for me. Some of those people were in the room that day, but thousands were not, were not able to hear how grateful I was, and how I feel, really, that I owe my life to them. Hopefully though, one day, they'll find this book in a library, or lying on a bus seat, or a friend will pick it up and tell them about it, and they will know.

✛ ✛ ✛

After the speech, I was so energized I wanted to walk all the way back to my office. I didn't think about how many steps it was. I just took off before anyone could tell me not to. That path back to the office is one I used to make multiple times a day, every day, and because I'm always late, usually I was running. On that day, every step was special. My face hurt from smiling so much. I was *moving*.

The sergeant at arms had roped off a pathway, so tourists had begun to gather along the rope line.

When I rounded the corner and hobble-crutched my way into Statuary Hall, a room with statues representing the giants of American democracy, I was given another one of the most special, emotional moments of my life.

By then, hundreds of people had crowded into the hall, crammed shoulder to shoulder against the rope line. Mixed in with them were reporters and photographers, but it was mostly tourists, people who'd come to see how their government works, to take in the rich history of democracy the building represents. People who just happened to have planned their family vacations for the same time I'd secretly decided to make my comeback.

In that moment, I remembered something about Statuary Hall. Congress actually used to meet there. They used to sit in front of those statues and hold their floor debates.

They moved a century and a half ago because it was too hard to conduct business in that space. When congressmen spoke, the room's curved ceiling amplified and distorted their words. It was too loud. People weren't hearing each other.

As I stood there leaning on my crutches, with a few hundred fellow citizens packed together, just for a brief moment, the room was silent.

For that moment, no one yelled. No one even spoke; no one needed to.

Somehow, we all understood better that way.

June 14th, 2018

EPILOGUE

It started, as most things do, as a joke. A bit I'd do in interviews.

When you're a member of Congress getting more press than you're used to, sometimes you lean on the same story or two, or certain jokes you know you can get a lot of mileage out of. Even the best of us aren't original all the time.

My joke was that I was going to play in the Congressional Baseball Game. As if I were a star player who'd just had an off year, I'd say, while sitting in the Geaux Kart or leaning on crutches, "I plan to go out there and compete for my job at second base."

I'm not sure interviewers found it funny, at least not after the first (or tenth) time, but I always laughed. It was my way of showing some good humor, that I was positive, that I hadn't lost the ability to be a little self-deprecating.

The more I said it out loud, though, the more the joke evolved. Not that it got funnier (obviously). It just went from a joke, to a fantasy, to the faint twinkling of a plan.

By the time practices for the game rolled around, almost a year after the shooting, walking on crutches actually *had* become second nature, and I was often able to move on just one crutch.

So, for kicks, in rehab, I asked my physical therapist, Katie, to get me ready for the game. She humored me, finding exercises I could actually do and that at least vaguely approximated the kind of training you'd do if you really were training to play baseball. She had me do exercises where I'd bend down, where I'd lean from side to side as if ground balls were coming at me, seeing how low down I could get, whether I could actually get low enough to pick up a ball. We did exercises with resistance bands attached to my ankles. Katie rolled balls to me, and I tried to reach over and pick them up, practicing coordination, stretching my muscles, making my body incrementally more flexible. I still had almost no lateral movement, but it was fun to practice, and dream, and pretend I was a Major Leaguer getting ready for the season.

As practices began again, I decided to go out and see my teammates. To carry on the tradition, if only symbolically. To get up earlier than I really wanted to, ride out in the car, listen to U2, see my friends, stand on the field, feel the air, feel the sun.

I even wobbled out to second base on my crutch a few times, threw the crutch behind me, and tried to take some grounders. And I like to think I did just as well as the other guys practicing at second base, at least with the grounders that came right to me. If they were over to the side I had no chance, but at least none of the ones coming at me went through my legs.

On the last day of practice, I rode out to the field, one last time. By coincidence, Dave Bailey was assigned to my security detail that morning, just as he had been on the morning, a year before, when all of our lives changed.

As we rode, I began to wonder if Dave knew what day it was. I wondered if he was thinking about it, too. We rode in silence for a while, and then, when I couldn't keep it to myself any more, I asked. "Dave," I said. "You know what today is?"

He turned around in his seat and considered me for a moment. Then he reached out his hand so I could give him a fist bump. For a moment, neither of us saying anything. Of course he knew what day it was.

✣ ✣ ✣

At that last practice, it seemed to me everyone on the team was thinking the same thing. They all knew what day it was, too; what had happened a year before, at this practice, on this day. Everyone was probably wound a little tighter than normal.

What if there was a copycat? A symbolic attack on the anniversary?

For all of those who still had some form of post-traumatic stress from the shooting, that morning was especially hard. Every sound and smell bore some connection to the day of the shooting. Everything threatened to set off a physiological response, like for the returning soldier who hears a car back-fire and whose mind goes back to war.

We were even looking at people around the field with suspicion. There was construction going on near the third baseline, and one worker just looked...a little *off.* There was something unsettling about the way he watched us. I realized one of the other players was staring at him, too.

"I don't like the look of that guy."

We were both fixated. It was easy to imagine a gunman around every corner. It was easy to feel the shooting could begin again, at any moment.

Perhaps sensing tension, Coach Williams sat us down in the dugout to read the starting lineup. As he went around the positions, reading off the starters, I had a moment, just like that day a decade before, when I expected to hear Brady's name read out for second base; instead, I heard my own.

I was overcome with emotion. Everyone cheered, everyone hugged.

Of course, it would just be symbolic; when game time came, I wouldn't stand out there for more than a play or two at most and wouldn't do anything but wave for a few seconds and then leave the field, but that didn't matter. I'd be there. I was fully aware in the instant I heard my name of what a perfect symbol of closure I'd been given—by God, by my friends on the team, by the doctors and nurses and paramedics who'd saved my life and rebuilt my body.

✠ ✠ ✠

As usual, I had to think about logistics.

How was I actually going to *get* out onto the field? I really didn't want to use the crutches. But still, a year later, I couldn't walk without them.

In the problem, however, there was an opportunity.

As I rode in the car, my mind moved to what I'd been thinking a lot about recently. It sounds trivial, but I'd been thinking about how baseball, a team sport, had brought us together, and when you think about it, even though it's just a game, it's a special exception in a town with an "every-man-for-himself" reputation. As Brad always points out, baseball is the only sport with a play called "the sacrifice." And of course, I was alive because of sacrifice. There were so many sacrifices that had allowed me to get to the point where I was actually going to be standing at second base again, even if only for a symbolic minute or two. Brad could have high-tailed it out of the park the moment gunfire erupted, but he stayed close so he could get to my side at the very first possible moment. Crystal and Dave didn't give a second thought to placing themselves in harm's way; they were willing to give up their lives if it meant others on that field wouldn't get hurt. I looked at Dave, up in front, riding shotgun, speaking quietly into his sleeve mic, his normal expression on his face, relaxed but alert, casual but aware, looking around, quietly taking it all in.

"Hey Dave," I said. "How would you feel about helping me walk out onto the field tonight?"

He was moved by the request. Of course, he said yes. And when he agreed, I called Crystal. She'd just had yet another surgery. She still wasn't back on field duty, even a year later, but she was able to move around in a walking boot. She agreed, too.

When the time came, that evening, after the national anthem, Dave came to me, and Crystal came to me, and they let me drape my arms around their shoulders.

Together, with my weight on them, the two people who'd taken bullets to save me helped me out to my position. The image of the three of us, arms draped around each other's backs, filled up the Jumbotron above us.

Dave and Crystal let me go, and I stood there at second base, under my own power, in the middle of Nationals Park. It felt like pure poetry, just standing there, feeling like I was really back. Feeling like something had been taken away from me, but now, was being given back.

✤ ✤ ✤

Just to be sure, I thought for a moment about who was coming up to bat. The first two batters were right-handers, so if either made contact, they'd be pulling the ball to the left side of the field, away from me, which meant I was safe. I could just stand there and enjoy the cheers, enjoy the moment, without any danger of anyone actually hitting a ball at me. I could just soak it in, stand out there on a warm but not too hot day, smiling, looking at all the people in the stands sharing this moment with me, and then the game was under way, North Carolina Congressman Mark Walker winding up and throwing the ball, Congressman Raul Ruiz twisting around and swinging, making contact, the ball pinging off the bat, racing along the ground... right at me.

You gotta be kidding!

And then, *I need to get this! There's no* way *I can miss this!*

In the split second it took to register what was happening, that the very first pitch was hit in my direction, I knew I couldn't screw it up. This whole moment depended on me. The ball was screaming at me, a little to my right. I still had no lateral movement, though! I still wasn't able to shimmy to my side. I had to find a way to get this big stiff body over to the right. I leaned to get in front of the ball, then leaned farther on my reconstructed pelvis, as the ball caught the dirt and kicked low, to my right. The ball skipped up into my glove—*Yes!*—then I realized I was going down—*No!* And then I was on the ground. I had the ball, but I'd fallen to one knee, with Ruiz barreling down the first base line toward Mo Brooks, who was playing first base and had his foot on the bag, *willing* me to get to the ball to him. In that moment, every sense in my body was heightened; my sense of feeling so elevated that I could feel, in my hands, tiny grains of dirt from the infield that had come up with the ball.

I knew that feeling.

A memory came tumbling into place.

As Ruiz barreled down the first baseline, my mind, for a split second, went elsewhere—the day of the shooting, gunfire over me, my hands digging into the dirt, desperately trying to pull myself away from the gunman, grabbing the ground so hard that days after I woke up, my palms would still be patterned with indentations from all of the tiny rocks that had embedded in them.

I tried to push the memory aside—*I cannot mess up this throw*—and with everything I had, while still on the ground, I swung my arm forward and let the ball go with as much force as I could get behind it. It seemed like an eternity, with Ruiz just steps away from the base.

Then, right before Ruiz got there, Mo caught the ball.

Just in time.

The umpire yelled, "Out!" and Mo pumped his fist. The crowd roared. Players started running toward me. Everyone on my team, from every position, was running toward me. I registered Jeff Duncan coming toward me from shortstop and, I realized, this moment must be especially meaningful for him because on the day of the shooting, he'd actually spoken to the gunman who asked him what team was practicing.

Duncan was with me, and then Democrats were running toward me, too. All of a sudden, it felt like *all* the players were with me, and I realized I was about to be at the bottom of a very big pile. I welled up with emotion. I was stunned. All I could think was, *This is not possible. This is not possible. What just happened is not possible.* In an instant the field was almost entirely empty, everyone charging toward second base. Ruiz, the player I'd thrown out, hadn't even bothered to finish his run to the base. The moment he was called out, he veered off the base path and ran right at me, wanting to congratulate me, to hug me, happy to have been a part of this moment, a moment that would have seemed absurd if you'd tried to make it up.

One batter later, Cedric was up, and I signaled to him before he went to the plate. It was time. It wasn't going to get any better (and I wanted my team to have a chance). I signaled to Brad Wenstrup, who was in the outfield behind me.

The two ran toward second base to get me, one player from each team. Two more people I'd depended on, Cedric for so many things over the years, for steady friendship perhaps most of all, and perspective; Brad for one very specific thing, for saving my life on the field.

The crowd was standing and cheering as I draped my arms over Cedric and Brad, let them take my weight, and we made our way back to the dugout.

As we walked, I could see, in the stands with all my staff and members of the cheering section, the team from the hospital. There was Dr. Sava, Susan Kennedy, Dr. Golden, my rehab doctor John Aseff, and my physical therapists Meaghan and Katie—all the people who'd helped me get back on my feet, back in the game, back to my life, all of them there for me still, all these people, a stadium full of people, each of them responsible, in some way big or small, for this moment. And I knew that here, in this country, with these people, that bullet never had a chance.

Acknowledgments

In addition to dedicating this book to my family, I want to acknowledge some other dear friends who helped save my life and get me back in the game!

To David Bailey, Crystal Griner, and all of our law enforcement officers who heroically and selflessly put their lives on the line every day: The outcome of June 14, 2017, would have been devastatingly different for everyone on that ballfield had you not been there and risked your lives for all of us.

To Colonel Brad Wenstrup, Dr. Jack Sava, and the countless other heroes who saved my life on the field and in the hospital: Your quick response and dedication that day, and in the days and weeks to come, brought me back from the brink of death.

The entire staff at MedStar Hospital, led by Susan Kennedy, make magic happen on a daily basis.

Dr. Rob Golden literally put me back together, and my physical therapists Meaghan Minzy and Katie Seward and occupational therapist Mandy Summers had the skill and patience to teach me how to walk again when some thought it might not be possible. You never gave up on me!

I wouldn't have made it through this without all of the family, friends, and complete strangers who offered their prayers and support to me and my family. Your acts of kindness and love lifted me up and gave me inspiration during the darkest days and carried me through this amazing journey.

And while I can't list everyone, I especially have to thank my sister Tara, Rick and Karen Legendre, and Charles Henry for spending countless days and nights with me and Jen.

Jennifer, you truly helped me pull so many pieces of this story together so that I could re-live some of the things that happened to me that I don't remember because I was on the brink of death. Your legendary notes that you took, day by day throughout my hospital stay (along with your revolving door of wonderful friends), were invaluable for us to tell this story in the right way.

Brett, you held the office together with a steady keel, even during the lowest moments, and you've been an invaluable sounding board for all of my ideas, good or bad.

And to my co-author, Jeff Stern, for lending your expertise to this project. Because this is the only book I've ever written, there is no way I could have made it work without your knowledge and professionalism. You helped me condense this last roller-coaster year into a structured outline that tells this near-tragic story, with its ultimately happy ending, in such a way that the reader feels they are there with us every step of the way.

About the Authors

Congressman Steve Scalise was elected to the US Congress in May 2008 after serving in the Louisiana legislature from 1996 to 2008. He currently serves as the Majority Whip, the third highest position for House Republicans. A native of Jefferson Parish, Louisiana, Scalise is a graduate of Archbishop Rummel High School and Louisiana State University, where he earned a degree in computer science with a minor in political science. Scalise is married to the former Jennifer Letulle, and they have two children, Madison and Harrison. He resides in Jefferson, Louisiana.

Jeffrey E. Stern is the author of *The Last Thousand: One School's Promise in a Nation at War* and the co-author of *The 15:17 to Paris*. A journalist and war correspondent, his reporting has appeared in *Vanity Fair, The Atlantic Monthly, The New York Times Magazine,* and elsewhere.